Lecture Notes in Computer Science 13782

More information about this series at https://link.springer.com/bookseries/558

Andrea Saracino · Paolo Mori (Eds.)

Emerging Technologies for Authorization and Authentication

5th International Workshop, ETAA 2022
Copenhagen, Denmark, September 30, 2022
Revised Selected Papers

 Springer

Editors
Andrea Saracino ⓘ
Istituto di Informatica e Telematica,
Consiglio Nazionale delle Ricerche
Pisa, Italy

Paolo Mori ⓘ
Istituto di Informatica e Telematica,
Consiglio Nazionale delle Ricerche
Pisa, Italy

ISSN 0302-9743   ISSN 1611-3349 (electronic)
Lecture Notes in Computer Science
ISBN 978-3-031-25466-6   ISBN 978-3-031-25467-3 (eBook)
https://doi.org/10.1007/978-3-031-25467-3

This Springer imprint is published by the registered company Springer Nature Switzerland AG
The registered company address is: Gewerbestrasse 11, 6330 Cham, Switzerland

Preface

This book contains the papers which were selected for presentation at the 5th International Workshop on Emerging Technologies for Authorization and Authentication (ETAA 2022), which was held in Darmstadt, Germany, on September 30, 2022, co-located with the 27th European Symposium on Research in Computer Security, (ESORICS 2022).

The workshop program included one invited paper and eight full papers concerning the workshop topics, in particular new techniques for biometric and behavioral-based authentication along with authentication and authorization in IoT and in distributed systems in general, including the Smart Home environment. All papers have been reviewed through a single blind review process. Every paper has been reviewed by 2 or 3 reviewers.

We would like to express our thanks to the invited speaker, to the authors who submitted their papers to the fifth edition of this workshop, thus contributing to making it again a successful event. We acknowledge the sponsorship and advertisement done by the EU-Funded H2020 SIFIS-Home project (GA number: 952652).

Last but not least, we would like to express our gratitude to the members of the Technical Program Committee for their valuable work in evaluating the submitted papers.

October 2022   Paolo Mori
                                                                          Andrea Saracino

Organization

Workshop Chairs

Paolo Mori   Consiglio Nazionale delle Ricerche, Italy
Andrea Saracino   Consiglio Nazionale delle Ricerche, Italy

Technical Program Committee

Benjamin Aziz	University of Portsmouth, UK
Francesco Di Cerbo	SAP Lab, France
Damiano Di Francesco Maesa	University of Pisa, Italy
Vasileios Gkioulos	Norwegian University of Science and Technology, Norway
Jens Jensen	Science and Technology Facilities Council, UK
Erisa Karafili	University of Southampton, UK
Georgios Karopulos	JRC, Italy
Mirko Manea	HPE Italia, Italy
Eleonora Losiouk	University of Padua, Italy
Silvio Ranise	University of Trento and Fondazione Bruno Kessler, Italy
Marco Rasori	Consiglio Nazionale delle Ricerche, Italy
Francesco Santini	University of Perugia, Italy
Marco Tiloca	RISE, Sweden

Contents

An Ontology-Based Approach for Setting Security Policies in Smart Homes

Alberto Monge Roffarello[✉] and Luigi De Russis

Politecnico di Torino, Corso Duca degli Abruzzi, 24, 10129 Turin, Italy
{alberto.monge,luigi.derussis}@polito.it

Abstract. To preserve the security and the integrity of smart home environments, a smart home system should provide end users with mechanisms to define security-based policies on their devices and services without the need to know (and specify) details that strongly depend on the underlying technology. To this end, this paper presents an End-User Development tool that allows users to a) define high-level security policies like *"do not record any sound in the living room tonight,"* b) check and debug high-level security policies against inconsistencies and redundancies, and c) translate high-level security policies into device-specific policies that can be applied at run-time. The tool implements a trigger-action programming paradigm, and it exploits a hybrid formalism based on ontologies and Petri Networks.

Keywords: End-user development · Internet of Things ·
Trigger-action programming · High-level policies

1 Introduction

The Internet of Things (IoT) is the paradigm whereby everyday objects are no longer disconnected from the virtual world, but they can be controlled remotely and serve as an access point to the Internet [29]. The advent of the IoT already helps society in many ways through applications ranging in scope from the individual to the planet [16]. People, in particular, can nowadays interact with a multitude of IoT devices in their homes: with lamps, thermostats, and many other appliances, including fridges and ovens, that can be connected to the Internet, homes are becoming "smart." Besides physical devices, many different online services, ranging from social networks to news and messaging apps, are greatly used by almost everyone: the number of people using the Internet passed 4.5 billion marks in January 2020, with more than 3.8 billion people actively using social media [33]. As a result, users can easily access a complex network of connected entities, be they smart devices or online services, that can communicate with each other, humans, and the environment.

The complexity of the IoT poses several security challenges, especially in the smart home context. Errors in automated behaviors, for example, can lead to unpredictable and dangerous behaviors [13]. While posting content on a social

© Springer Nature Switzerland AG 2023
A. Saracino and P. Mori (Eds.): ETAA 2022, LNCS 13782, pp. 1–14, 2023.
https://doi.org/10.1007/978-3-031-25467-3_1

network twice could be considered a trivial issue, wrong automation could unexpectedly unlock the main door of a house, thus generating a security threat. To preserve the security and the integrity of smart home environments, a smart home system should provide end users with mechanisms to define security-based high-level policies on their devices and services, without the need to know (and specify) details that strongly depend on the underlying technology. Following this need, this work proposes the Policy Translation Point (PTP) system, an end-user development tool that aims to support users to express high-level policies like *"Do not record sound in the living room tonight."* To this end, PTP uses an ontological representation for end-user development and employs a trigger-action programming paradigm through which high-level security policies are expressed as abstract trigger-action rules. These policies ultimately ensure that the behavior of the devices and applications involved in a given smart home adheres to the latest underlying policy description. In particular, PTP can translate high-level policies into device-level policies, when possible. Stemming from a high-level policy, for instance, the system could limit the features of a smart home device or inhibit the operation of a non-reconfigurable device. In addition, it could verify whether a given home configuration is compatible with one or more active (or suggested) policies. Besides empowering users to define and translate rules, PTP is also able to detect potential conflicts between high-level policies, namely redundancies (i.e., policies that produce equal or overlapping results) and inconsistencies (i.e., policies with contradictory actions).

2   Related Work

Smart home is an emerging application paradigm that has been gaining popularity in the last few years. Most recently, the IoT has fostered a vision of smart home systems, where users can install smart devices and applications that cooperate to manage home services and functionalities automatically. This emerging market rapidly attracts software developers to produce novel applications and services to provide additional smart home functionalities. However, noticeable barriers and concerns are still present, mainly related to cyber-security and safety within smart home systems, as well as to the privacy and integrity of produced and consumed data, most of which are personal and sensitive. In our work, we aim to design and implement a solution allowing end users to specify, debug, and translate high-level security policies that can be applied in a given smart home. This section contextualizes our work by discussing state-of-the-art literature on End-User Development (EUD) and rules modeling and analysis.

2.1   End-User Development in the IoT

Lieberman et al. [28] define End-User Development (EUD) as *"a set of methods, techniques, and tools that allow users of software systems, who are acting as non-professional software developers, at some point to create, modify or extend a software artifact."* With the technological advances we are confronting today, people are increasingly moving from passive consumers to active producers of information, data, and software [31], and EUD approaches and methodologies have been extensively explored in different contexts, e.g., mobile environments [32], smart homes [12,36], and web mashups [20,34]. The explosion of the IoT further increased the need to allow end users to customize the behavior of their smart devices and online services. One of the most popular paradigms to empower end users in directly programming their connected entities is trigger-action programming [22,36]. Trigger-action programming offers a straightforward and easy-to-learn solution for creating end-user applications, according to Barricelli and Valtolina [10]. It is not surprising that, in the last years, several commercial trigger-action programming platforms were born to allow end-user personalization of connected entities. Examples include IFTTT [2], Zapier [6], Microsoft Flow [3], Mozzilla's Thing Gateway [5], SmartRules [4], and many others. In its basic form, trigger-action programming allows users to connect a single event to a single action: by defining trigger-action (IF-THEN) rules, users can connect a pair of devices or online services in such a way that, when an event (the *trigger*) is detected on one of them, an *action* is automatically executed on the latter. Although some behaviors would require greater expressiveness to be defined in a single rule, e.g., through multiple actions or additional trigger conditions, many of the most popular trigger-action programming platforms, e.g., IFTTT, Zapier, and Microsoft Flow, still continue to adopt the basic form of the trigger-action programming paradigm [11].

Given its advantages and widespread adoption in EUD solutions for IoT environments, including smart homes, we decided to adopt the trigger-action programming paradigm to empower end users to define high-level security policies. Our approach is inspired by the work described in [19],in which the authors proposed a method based on Semantic Web technologies to express abstract (high-lelvel) trigger-action rules that adapt to different contextual situations, e.g., *"increase the home temperature when I'm coming home."*

2.2 Rule Modeling and Analysis

Despite the trigger-action programming paradigm can express most of the behaviors desired by potential users [10,36], and is adopted by the most common EUD platforms [21], the definition of trigger-action rules can be difficult for non-programmers. Multiple studies investigated different aspects of contemporary platforms like IFTTT, ranging from empirical characterization of the performance and usage of IFTTT [30] to human factors related to their adoption in the smart home [36]. Large-scale analysis of publicly shared rules on IFTTT [35], and changes to the underlying models are proposed as well [17,21]. In these studies, in particular, conflicts and ambiguities among rules emerged as possible challenges [36]. As a result, users frequently misinterpret the behavior of trigger-action rules [13], often deviating from their actual semantics, and are prone to introduce errors [24].

All the described problems naturally apply to the context of high-level security policies expressed as trigger-action rules. Consequently, our work also aims to allow users to check and debug their policies. Many prior works face the problem of formally or semi-formally verifying event-based rules with different approaches, especially in the area of databases [23,27], expert systems [38], and smart environments [8,37]. Rules, indeed, can interact with each other, and even a small set of dependencies between them makes it hard (and often undecidable) the problem of predicting their overall behavior [9]. Li et al. [27], for instance, propose a Conditional Colored Petri Net (CCPN) formalism to model and simulate Event-Condition-Action (ECA) rules for active databases. Petri nets are used by Yang et al. [38] to verify rules in expert systems, and by Jin et al. [26] to dynamically verify ECA properties such as termination and confluence. In the field of smart environments, Vannucchi et al. [37] adopt formal verification methods for ECA rules, while Augusto and Hornos [8] propose a methodological guide to use the Spin model checker to inform the development of more reliable, intelligent environments.

Most of the works described above aim to check the consistency of a set of fixed and *already* defined rules, not in real time, and employ predefined use cases to validate the algorithms. The goal of the PTP system is different. Instead of performing such an "off-line" verification of rules, PTP aims at assisting end users *during* the definition of their own security policies. For this purpose, we empower the PTP interface with a novel Petri net formalism, similar to CCPN but enhanced with new elements and with semantic information.

3   The Policy Translation Point System

The Policy Translation Point (PTP) is a system that has three main goals:

1. supporting users to express high-level security policies like *"Do not record sound in the living room tonight"*;
2. translating high-level security policies into device-level policies, when possible;
3. detecting potential conflicts between high-level security policies.

Figure 1 shows the client-server architecture of the PTP system. Through the web-based PTP User Interface, users can compose new high-level security policies. The PTP Server analyzes these policies taking into account the devices and applications installed in the smart home, and produces alarms in case of conflicts and/or translates the defined high-level policies into a set of device-level policies expressed in the XACML formalism [7].

In this Section, we present the models and formalisms adopted in the PTP system (Sect. 3.1), and we detail how users can compose and check high-level security policies through the PTP User Interface (Sect. 3.2). Finally, Sect. 3.3 presents the implementation details.

3.1   Adopted Models and Formalisms

Concept Modeling and Translation: The SIFIS-Home Ontology. The PTP system uses the SIFIS-Home ontology to model high-level security policies,

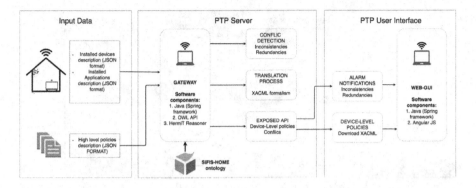

Fig. 1. The architecture of the PTP system.

smart home devices/applications, and users. Figure 2 shows the architecture of the SIFIS-Home ontology. We designed and implemented it by exploiting state-of-the-art vocabularies like foaf [1] and EUPont [19]. EUPont, in particular, is a high-level ontological representation of trigger-action programming that describes smart devices and online services based on their categories and capabilities, i.e., their offered services. In detail, for each trigger or action, the ontology provides information about the device or online service by which they are offered, and any relationship with other triggers or actions, e.g., the fact that an action implicitly activates a given trigger. Furthermore, triggers and actions are classified through a tree of classes that represents the final behavior they monitor, in case of triggers, or produce, in case of actions. Triggers or actions that are classified under the same EUPont classes, in particular, are similar in terms of final functionality, while triggers or actions that do not share any EUPont class are functionally contradictory. For example, the two actions *"set the Nest thermostat to Home mode"* and *"set 25 Celsius degree on the Nest thermostat"* share the same final functionality, because they are both classified under the same EUPont class, i.e., *IncreaseTemperature-Action*. Compared to these actions, the action *"set the Nest thermostat to Away mode"* is contradictory in terms of functionality, because it is classified under a different EUPont class, i.e., *DecreaseTemperatureAction*.

In our work, we specialized the EUPont classes to the context of high-level security policies in the smart home context. Each policy follows a simple trigger-action programming paradigm, and is defined through an abstract trigger-action rule composed of a single trigger and a single action. In the initial version of the SIFIS-Home ontology, we included the following triggers and actions:

- *Temporal triggers*: events that fire every morning, afternoon, evening, or night, respectively.
- *Video actions*: actions that allow or forbid video recording in a given location, e.g., the bedroom.
- *Audio actions*: actions that allow or forbid audio recording in a given location, e.g., the bedroom.

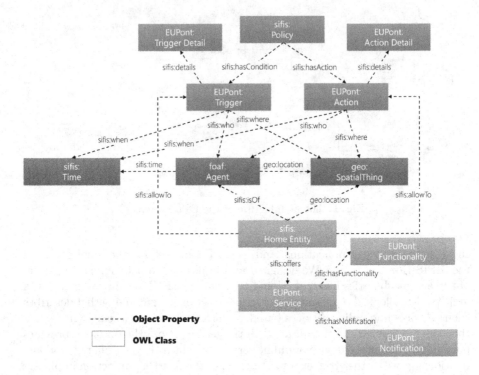

Fig. 2. The architecture of the SIFIS-Home ontology.

Figure 3a shows how a policy is modeled inside the SIFIS-Home ontology. The OWL class POLICY has two subclasses, i.e., TRIGGER and **ACTION**. A set of OWL restrictions have been added to specify that a policy must have a single trigger and a single action. Following the EUPont model, the TRIGGER and ACTION classes are in turn specialized in a hierarchy of OWL sub-classes representing events and actions of different categories. These hierarchies of sub-classes are expressed at different levels of abstraction: this potentially allows users to specify high-level policies in different ways, by choosing to be more or less specific. Figure 3b exemplifies some video-related actions included in the initial version of the SIFIS-Home ontology. For example, the SIFIS dont-record-video action is a RDFS instance of the STOP VIDEO class, while the SIFIS record-video action is a RDFS instance of the START VIDEO class.

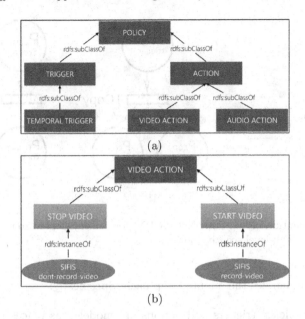

Fig. 3. Modeling of a policy inside the SIFIS-Home ontology.

As shown in Fig. 2, each trigger and action is directly linked with contextual information, e.g., locations (`SpatialThing`) and users (`Agent`), and indirectly linked with devices and applications installed in the smart home (`Home Entity`). PTP uses this information to translate the defined high-level policies into the corresponding set of device-level policies in the XACML formalism.

Conflicts Detection: Semantic Colored Petri Nets. To model and check the behavior of high-level security policies at run-time, we defined a formalism inspired by the Semantic Colored Petri Net (SCPN) approach defined in [18]. Petri nets are bipartite directed graphs, in which directed arcs connect places and transitions. Places may hold tokens, which are used to study the dynamic behavior of the net. They can naturally describe policies expressed as trigger-action rules as well as their non-deterministic concurrent environment [26]. We chose such an approach to allow users to simulate step-by-step the execution of their policies: by firing a transition at a time, tokens move in the net by giving the idea of a possible execution flow. As a member of Petri nets family, Colored Petri Nets (CPNs) [25] combine the strengths of ordinary Petri nets with the strengths of a high-level programming language. In particular, SCPN is a Colored Petri Net similar to the Conditional Colored Petri Net (CCPN) formalism [27] proposed to model ECA rules in active databases. Differently from such a formalism, we do not consider conditions and use a semantic model to generate and analyze the net. Furthermore, each token assumes different semantic "colors" by moving in the net: places, in particular, are labeled with the corresponding OWL classes extracted from the SIFIS-Home ontology. Such semantic information allows the inference of more information from the simulation of the net, i.e., to discriminate between problematic and safe policies.

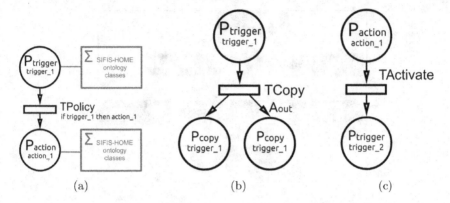

Fig. 4. The Semantic Colored Petri Net (SCPN) formalism adopted to model the run-time behavior of high-level security policies.

Figure 4 summarizes the adopted approach. Specifically:

- High-level policies' triggers and actions are modeled as places in the Petri Net. When a trigger is in common between more than one policy, the associated places are duplicated and connected through a dedicated copy transition (*TCopy*, Fig. 4a). When a token is in the original place, the copy transition simply replicates the token in each copied place. Instead, action places can be directly reused by policies that have the same action.
- Places can be connected each other through a policy transition (*TPolicy*, Fig. 4a), i.e., a connection between the trigger and the action of the same policy, or through an activate transition (*TActivate*, Fig. 4c), i.e., a connection used when an action of a high-level policy triggers the event of another high-level policy.
- Places, i.e., high-level policies' triggers and actions, are labeled with the corresponding OWL classes extracted from the SIFIS-Home ontology (Fig. 4a).

Using the described model, PTP is able to detect two possible conflicts among the currently available high-level policies: inconsistencies and redundancies.

Inconsistencies occur when policies that should be activated at (nearly) the same time[1] try to execute contradictory actions. In trigger-action rules, an inconsistency occurs when the execution order of rules may render different final states in the system [15]. In this work, we generalized this concept to consider the entire smart-home ecosystem, i.e., not only physical devices but also online services. For this reason, we analyze the *meaning* of the actions executed by the involved policies rather than their execution order. An example of a set of policies that produces an inconsistency is:

- *when* in the morning, from 9 to 12 AM, *then* record video in the bedroom;

---

[1] e.g., when policies share the same trigger or when some policies trigger other policies.

- *when* in the morning, from 9 to 12 AM, *then* do not record any video in the bedroom;

Here, the two policies are executed simultaneously because they share the same trigger and produce two contradictory actions, i.e., allowing and prohibiting video recording in the bedroom.

Redundancies, instead, occur when two or more policies that are activated (nearly) at the same time have replicated functionality [15]. An example of a set of policies that produce a redundancy is:

- *when* in the evening, from 6 to 9 PM, *then* do not record any audio in the entire home;
- *when* in the evening, from 6 to 9 PM, *then* do not record any audio in the living room.

Also in this case, the two policies are executed simultaneously because they share the same trigger. Here, however, the action of the second policy is redundant with the action of the first policy, as the living room is part of the entire home.

3.2   User Interface

The PTP user interface can be logically split into three parts: a) *Policy Composition* (Fig. 5), b) *Problem Checking* (Fig. 6a), and c) *Step-by-Step Explanation* (Fig. 6b). The Problem Checking and the Step-by-Step Explanation interfaces implement two well-known end-user debugging strategies: identification of rule conflicts and simulation of the run-time behavior.

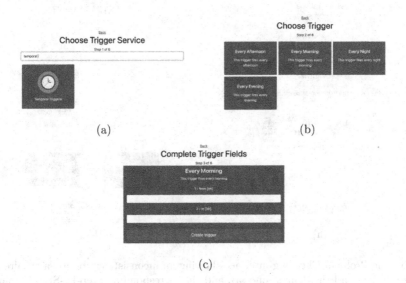

Fig. 5. The definition of a new high-level security policy in the PTP interface.

To allow the composition of high-level security policies, we designed a user interface based on the form-filling paradigm, an approach that has been found to be effective and easy to use in trigger-action programming platforms by several previous works, e.g., [14, 21]. In addition, the form-filling procedure it adopts helps users to avoid syntactical errors during the composition process. To compose a policy, a user must first select which service they want to use as a trigger, e.g., "Temporal Triggers" (Fig. 5a). Once they select a service, they can choose the specific trigger to be used (e.g., "Every Morning," Fig. 5b) and fill in any additional information required by the trigger (e.g., the specific time interval, Fig. 5c). To define the action part of the rule, the user has to repeat the same steps.

When a rule has been composed, PTP uses the mechanisms described in Sect. 3.1 to find any possible conflicts with the policies that have been defined in the past, highlighting a problem to the user if necessary. The *Problem Checking* interface, in particular, shows the policy just defined by the user and any problems that the policy may generate. In Fig. 6a, for instance, a possible inconsistency between two policies is highlighted. To better understand the problems and to foresee the run-time behavior of the involved policies, the user can click on the "Explanation" button to open the *Step-by-Step Explanation* interface (Fig. 6b). In such an interface, the user can simulate step-by-step what happens within their policies, to try to understand why the highlighted problems arise.

At the end of the composition procedure, if no problems are detected, the user has the possibility to translate the defined high-level policy into a set of XACML policies.

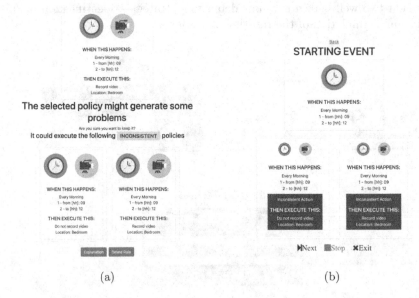

| (a) | (b) |

Fig. 6. The Problem Checking interface showing an inconsistency between an already existent policy and the defined one (a), and the corresponding Step-by-Step Explanation (b).

3.3 Implementation

The implementation of the PTP system consists of two main components:

PTP Server It is built in Java with the Spring framework[2]. It is composed of three modules: *Policy Service*, *SCPN Service*, and *Policy Controller*. The Policy Service offers the features needed to manage collections of policies i.e., to create, read, update, and delete policies through the interaction with a MySQL database. Once a user has completed a policy, the SCPN Service generates and analyzes the SCPN by retrieving the defined policies from the Policy Service, and by using the OWL API[3] library to extract the needed semantic information from the SIFIS-Home ontology. The same module is also responsible for the step-by-step simulation of the involved policies. Finally, the Policy Controller exposes a list of REST APIs to interact with the two services.

PTP User Interface It is the web-based interface built with the Angular framework[4]. It interacts with the PTP Server through the provided REST APIs.

4 Conclusions

In this paper, we have presented the Policy Translation Point system, and End-User Development tool that empowers users to define, translate, and debug high-level security policies. The tool exploits a novel formalism based on Semantic Web technologies and Petri Nets, and it implements a trigger-action programming approach through which users can define policies as abstract trigger-action rules that do not depend on any specific technology. Furthermore, it is able to detect redundancies and inconsistencies between high-level security policies, and it can translate a high-level policy into a set of XACML policies that can be directly applied to the devices and applications installed in the smart home.

Acknowledgments. The work described in this paper is part of the SIFIS-Home Project that is supported by funding under the Horizon 2020 Framework Program of the European Commission SU-ICT-02-2020 GA 952652.

References

1. FOAF vocabulary specification (2004). http://xmlns.com/foaf/0.1/. Accessed 07 Nov 2022
2. IFTTT (2019). https://ifttt.com/. Accessed 20 Nov 2019
3. Microsoft flow (2019). https://flow.microsoft.com/en-us/. Accessed 20 Nov 2019
4. Smartrules (2019). http://smartrulesapp.com/. Accessed 20 Nov 2019

---

[2] https://spring.io, last visited on November 07, 2022.

[3] http://owlapi.sourceforge.net, last visited November 07, 2022.

[4] https://angular.io, last visited on November 07, 2022.

5. Webthings gateway (2019). https://iot.mozilla.org/gateway/. Accessed 20 Nov 2019
6. Zapier (2019). https://zapier.com/. Accessed 20 Nov 2019
7. Oasis extensible access control markup language (XACML) TC (2020). https://www.oasis-open.org/committees/tc_home.php?wg_abbrev=xacml. Accessed 07 Nov 2022
8. Augusto, J.C., Hornos, M.J.: Software simulation and verification to increase the reliability of intelligent environments. Adv. Eng. Softw. **58**(Suppl. C), 18–34 (2013). https://doi.org/10.1016/j.advengsoft.2012.12.004
9. Bailey, J., Dong, G., Ramamohanarao, K.: On the decidability of the termination problem of active database systems. Theoret. Comput. Sci. **311**(1), 389–437 (2004). https://doi.org/10.1016/j.tcs.2003.09.003
10. Barricelli, B.R., Valtolina, S.: Designing for end-user development in the internet of things. In: Díaz, P., Pipek, V., Ardito, C., Jensen, C., Aedo, I., Boden, A. (eds.) IS-EUD 2015. LNCS, vol. 9083, pp. 9–24. Springer, Cham (2015). https://doi.org/10.1007/978-3-319-18425-8_2
11. Brackenbury, W., et al.: How users interpret bugs in trigger-action programming. In: Proceedings of the 2019 CHI Conference on Human Factors in Computing Systems, CHI 2019, pp. 552:1–552:12. ACM, New York (2019). https://doi.org/10.1145/3290605.3300782
12. Brich, J., Walch, M., Rietzler, M., Weber, M., Schaub, F.: Exploring end user programming needs in home automation. ACM Trans. Comput.-Hum. Interact. **24**(2), 11:1–11:35 (2017). https://doi.org/10.1145/3057858
13. Brush, A.B., Lee, B., Mahajan, R., Agarwal, S., Saroiu, S., Dixon, C.: Home automation in the wild: challenges and opportunities. In: Proceedings of the SIGCHI Conference on Human Factors in Computing Systems, CHI 2011, pp. 2115–2124. ACM, New York (2011). https://doi.org/10.1145/1978942.1979249
14. Caivano, D., Fogli, D., Lanzilotti, R., Piccinno, A., Cassano, F.: Supporting end users to control their smart home: design implications from a literature review and an empirical investigation. J. Syst. Softw. **144**, 295–313 (2018). https://doi.org/10.1016/j.jss.2018.06.035
15. Cano, J., Delaval, G., Rutten, E.: Coordination of ECA rules by verification and control. In: Kühn, E., Pugliese, R. (eds.) COORDINATION 2014. LNCS, vol. 8459, pp. 33–48. Springer, Heidelberg (2014). https://doi.org/10.1007/978-3-662-43376-8_3
16. Cerf, V., Senges, M.: Taking the internet to the next physical level. IEEE Comput. **49**(2), 80–86 (2016). https://doi.org/10.1109/MC.2016.51
17. Corno, F., De Russis, L., Monge Roffarello, A.: A semantic web approach to simplifying trigger-action programming in the IoT. Computer **50**(11), 18–24 (2017). https://doi.org/10.1109/MC.2017.4041355
18. Corno, F., De Russis, L., Monge Roffarello, A.: Empowering end users in debugging trigger-action rules. In: Proceedings of the 2019 CHI Conference on Human Factors in Computing Systems, CHI 2019, pp. 1–13. Association for Computing Machinery, New York (2019). https://doi.org/10.1145/3290605.3300618
19. Corno, F., De Russis, L., Monge Roffarello, A.: A high-level semantic approach to end-user development in the internet of things. Int. J. Hum.-Comput. Stud. **125**(C), 41–54 (2019). https://doi.org/10.1016/j.ijhcs.2018.12.008
20. Daniel, F., Matera, M.: Mashups: Concepts, Models and Architectures. Springer, Heidelberg (2014). https://doi.org/10.1007/978-3-642-55049-2

21. Desolda, G., Ardito, C., Matera, M.: Empowering end users to customize their smart environments: model, composition paradigms, and domain-specific tools. ACM Trans. Comput.-Hum. Interact. **24**(2), 12:1–12:52 (2017). https://doi.org/10.1145/3057859

22. Dey, A.K., Sohn, T., Streng, S., Kodama, J.: iCAP: interactive prototyping of context-aware applications. In: Fishkin, K.P., Schiele, B., Nixon, P., Quigley, A. (eds.) Pervasive 2006. LNCS, vol. 3968, pp. 254–271. Springer, Heidelberg (2006). https://doi.org/10.1007/11748625_16

23. Gatziu, S., Dittrich, K.R.: Detecting composite events in active database systems using petri nets. In: Proceedings of IEEE International Workshop on Research Issues in Data Engineering: Active Databases Systems, pp. 2–9 (1994). https://doi.org/10.1109/RIDE.1994.282859

24. Huang, J., Cakmak, M.: Supporting mental model accuracy in trigger-action programming. In: Proceedings of the 2015 ACM International Joint Conference on Pervasive and Ubiquitous Computing, UbiComp 2015, pp. 215–225. ACM, New York (2015). https://doi.org/10.1145/2750858.2805830

25. Jensen, K.: Coloured Petri Nets: Basic Concepts, Analysis Methods and Practical Use, vol. 2. Springer, London (1995)

26. Jin, X., Lembachar, Y., Ciardo, G.: Symbolic termination and confluence checking for ECA rules. In: Koutny, M., Haddad, S., Yakovlev, A. (eds.) Transactions on Petri Nets and Other Models of Concurrency IX. LNCS, vol. 8910, pp. 99–123. Springer, Heidelberg (2014). https://doi.org/10.1007/978-3-662-45730-6_6

27. Li, X., Medina, J.M., Chapa, S.V.: Applying petri nets in active database systems. IEEE Trans. Syst. Man Cybern. Part C (Appl. Rev.) **37**(4), 482–493 (2007). https://doi.org/10.1109/TSMCC.2007.897329

28. Lieberman, H., Paternò, F., Klann, M., Wulf, V.: End-user development: an emerging paradigm. In: Lieberman, H., Paternó, F., Wulf, V. (eds.) End User Development, pp. 1–8. Springer, Dordrecht (2006). https://doi.org/10.1007/1-4020-5386-X_1

29. Mattern, F., Floerkemeier, C.: From the internet of computers to the internet of things. In: Sachs, K., Petrov, I., Guerrero, P. (eds.) From Active Data Management to Event-Based Systems and More. LNCS, vol. 6462, pp. 242–259. Springer, Heidelberg (2010). https://doi.org/10.1007/978-3-642-17226-7_15

30. Mi, X., Qian, F., Zhang, Y., Wang, X.: An empirical characterization of IFTTT: ecosystem, usage, and performance. In: Proceedings of the 2017 Internet Measurement Conference, IMC 2017, pp. 398–404. ACM, New York (2017). https://doi.org/10.1145/3131365.3131369

31. Munjin, D.: User empowerment in the internet of things. Ph.D. thesis, Université de Genève (2013). http://archive-ouverte.unige.ch/unige:28951

32. Namoun, A., Daskalopoulou, A., Mehandjiev, N., Xun, Z.: Exploring mobile end user development: existing use and design factors. IEEE Trans. Software Eng. **42**(10), 960–976 (2016). https://doi.org/10.1109/TSE.2016.2532873

33. We are Social Digital in 2020 (2020). https://wearesocial.com/blog/2020/01/digital-2020-3-8-billion-people-use-social-media

34. Stolee, K.T., Elbaum, S.: Identification, impact, and refactoring of smells in pipe-like web mashups. IEEE Trans. Software Eng. **39**(12), 1654–1679 (2013). https://doi.org/10.1109/TSE.2013.42

35. Ur, B., et al.: Trigger-action programming in the wild: an analysis of 200,000 IFTTT recipes. In: Proceedings of the 34rd Annual ACM Conference on Human Factors in Computing Systems, CHI 2016, pp. 3227–3231. ACM, New York (2016). https://doi.org/10.1145/2858036.2858556

36. Ur, B., McManus, E., Pak Yong Ho, M., Littman, M.L.: Practical trigger-action programming in the smart home. In: Proceedings of the SIGCHI Conference on Human Factors in Computing Systems, CHI 2014, pp. 803–812. ACM, New York (2014). https://doi.org/10.1145/2556288.2557420
37. Vannucchi, C., et al.: Symbolic verification of event–condition–action rules in intelligent environments. J. Reliab. Intell. Environ. **3**(2), 117–130 (2017). https://doi.org/10.1007/s40860-017-0036-z
38. Yang, S.J.H., Lee, A.S., Chu, W.C., Yang, H.: Rule base verification using petri nets. In: Proceedings of the Twenty-Second Annual International Computer Software and Applications Conference, COMPSAC 1998, pp. 476–481 (1998). https://doi.org/10.1109/CMPSAC.1998.716699

ClapAuth: A Gesture-Based User-Friendly Authentication Scheme to Access a Secure Infrastructure

Attaullah Buriro$^{(\boxtimes)}$ (iD) and Francesco Ricci

Faculty of Computer Science, Free University of Bolzano, Bolzano, Italy
{aburiro,fricci}@unibz.it

Abstract. In this paper we propose a gesture-based user-friendly smartwatch-based user authentication scheme called ClapAuth to authenticate the users to gain physical access to a secure infrastructure. In ClapAuth users are authenticated by performing clapping actions, while wearing their smartwatch in one hand. ClapAuth, while users perform clapping gestures, profiles them by collecting data from their smartwatches' built-in accelerometer and gyroscope sensors. We have evaluated the proposed scheme on a publicly available dataset by using state-of-the-art n-class machine learning classifiers, namely Random Forest (RF), Artificial Neural Network (ANN), and K-Nearest Neighbors (KNN). KNN outperformed other two classifiers and attained 93.3% TAR at the cost of 0.22% FAR. ClapAuth could be widely accepted as it utilizes users' familiarity with a common action, such as clapping, and users are not required to remember any secret code or gesture.

Keywords: Biometrics · Authentication and access control · Behavioral biometrics · Smartwatch

1 Introduction

Computer technology, and especially cyber technology involving Internet or cyberspace, is not just limited to electronic and computing devices, it could also be evaluated in securing access to secure facilities. The introduction of computing and communication capabilities combined with machine learning is not only making such facilities "smart" [1], but also secure. The main goal of this paper is to control the access to a smart facility, i.e., an office building or smart home. Existing approaches to secure access control mainly rely on some form of physical device, i.e., locks, doors, or barriers, which must be reliable but also acceptable for the users [2]. Needless to say, these physical access control systems are evolving in terms of technology but also in terms of user authentication schemes.

Most of the lock manufactures, for example [3], offer PIN/password-based schemes, device-pairing (with smartcards, smartphones), and physical biometrics (using face, fingerprints), as it is depicted in Fig. 1. However, these schemes

© Springer Nature Switzerland AG 2023
A. Saracino and P. Mori (Eds.): ETAA 2022, LNCS 13782, pp. 15–30, 2023.
https://doi.org/10.1007/978-3-031-25467-3_2

have shown to be insecure, as they are vulnerable to various attacks [4], and not usable [5,6]. Furthermore, a recent study [7] reports that 55% of the participants prefer password-less access, 50% of them used to share their passwords with others, and 62% of them consider second-factor authentication as annoying. Similarly, 65% of interviewed users consider biometrics as a better approach (as they say it would increase the security), however, 30% of them had serious privacy concerns in sharing their biometric data. These limitations motivate the design of gesture-based usable metaphors for smartwatches and physical access control systems using behavioral biometrics.

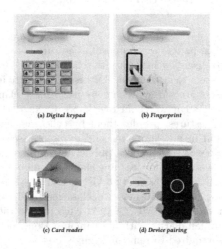

(a) *Digital keypad*   (b) *Fingerprint*

(c) *Card reader*   (d) *Device pairing*

Fig. 1. User Authentication schemes on existing smart locks [28]

Smartwatches besides their traditional use (e.g., showing time, managing text messages and phone calls), are now used to perform sensitive operations, i.e., opening the garage doors[1] and accessing cars[2], just to name a few. To this end, we intend to use behavioral-biometric-powered smartwatch as a key to access the secure infrastructure.

Behavioral biometric, e.g., swiping and touch-dynamics, seems a better option for the development of gesture-based user authentication schemes mainly because: (i) their data can be collected transparently, (ii) data collection does not require any additional hardware, (iii) they are secure, and (iv) unlike physical biometrics, they offer the possibility to easily revoking the compromised behavioral attributes. Since, behavioral biometrics are dependent on the user actions and habits, it makes them more suited to frictionless and unobtrusive user authentication [8]. Behavioral biometrics exploit continuously collected person-specific data, by common smartphone/smartwatch sensors, to profile users. Several unique behavioral

---

[1] https://www.iphoneness.com/home-automation-2/apple-watch-garage-door-opener/.

[2] https://www.macworld.com/article/676033/bmw-to-use-iphones-u1-chip-for-digital-car-keys.html.

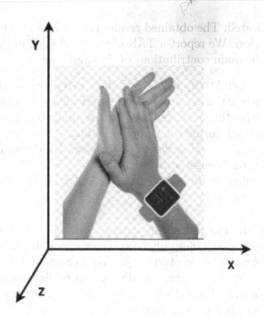

Fig. 2. Clapping gesture in 3D space

features (differently from static biometrics), e.g., swiping/typing speed, finger size/pressure, etc., are collected to create a unique profile of the user. Additionally, the inherent capability of liveness detection (without initiating any challenge) makes behavioral biometrics preferable over their above mentioned counterparts. As a result, researchers in the authentication domain started designing behavioral biometric-based schemes, such as, swiping [9], typing [10–12], gait [13], and arm-movements [14].

In this paper, we present a friction less and user-friendly hands-clapping gesture-based user authentication scheme - CLAPAUTH, for smartwatch. CLAPAUTH, while the user performs a clapping gesture (as depicted in Fig. 2), collects arm movements data by means of the user's smartwatch accelerometer and gyroscope sensor, and it uses this data for user profiling. More specifically CLAPAUTH collects the arm-movement generated data, from accelerometer and gyroscope for the entire duration of the clapping gesture and executes identity confirmation. CLAPAUTH, by using the proper Machine Learning classification techniques decides if the smartwatch is worn by the legitimate user or by an impostor. Access to the secure facility is granted in case the user is confirmed as legitimate user, otherwise it is denied. CLAPAUTH neither requires any token, password, nor any extra user-effort for authentication, thus, making it completely friction less and usable for access to a secure facility. We framed the problem of accessing secure facility as an n-class classification problem where the classifier is trained on samples of several users, hosted on a centralized server. Here, the decision is made on the server, and access to the facility is granted only when the user is authenticated. The obtained results prove CLAPAUTH as an effective authentication solution. We report a TAR of 93.3% at FAR of 0.22%.

In conclusion, the main contributions of this paper are:

- The proposal of CLAPAUTH - a smartwatch-powered arm-motion-based user-friendly user authentication scheme for physical access control. The proposed scheme authenticates users based on the analysis of the captured arm-movements generated during the clapping action.
- The investigation and evaluation of that novel hand-clapping gesture as behavioral-biometric for user authentication.
- The proof of excellent performance of CLAPAUTH, which achieves a TAR of 93.3% at FAR of 0.22%.

Paper Organization. The rest of the paper is organized as follows: Sect. 2 surveys the relevant research studies published for smartwatch unlocking. Section 3 presents a high-level explanation of our approach. In Sect. 4 we present the evaluation strategy and analysis. In Sect. 5 we discuss our findings and the limitations of our proposed scheme. We conclude this work with a summary of our findings and by identifying future works in Sect. 6.

2   Related Work

2.1   Behavioral-Biometric-Based Smartwatch User Authentication

Knowledge-based one-time authentication schemes are not shown to be a preferred choice because of their well-known and its well documented security and usability issues. Static biometric, e.g., face, fingerprint, could somehow address these problems, however, as mentioned earlier, it also has security, usability, and privacy concerns. Thus, the need for novel behavioral biometric-based schemes is observed.

Smartwatches are now fitted with sensors that could detect wrist rotations, arm movements, finger gestures, heart-rate, blood oxygen level, skin temperature and conductance. This information can be utilized for implicit user authentication. Behavioral biometric-based user authentication on smartwatches is comparatively a less-explored area. Researchers have exploited taping [15], swiping [16], motion-assisted [17–24] modalities for authentication.

Draw-a-pin [15] leverages the drawing behavior of a user and the correctness of the drawn PIN, to authenticate the user. Authors achieved 4.84% average error rate on their collected dataset of 30 participants, in two activities, i.e., sitting, walking, in-lab settings using Samsung Gear Live smartwatch.

Lewis et al [18] proposed a motion-based authentication solution for smartwatch users. The system exploits the free-form arm-movement as behavioral biometric modality for user authentication. By applying a Dynamic Time Warping (DTW) classifier on their collected dataset of 5 users, authors achieved accuracy up to 84.6%, depending on the experimental settings. Similarly, in another relevant study, namely "VeriNET", the authors take motion signals as password, and use a deep recurrent neural network to authenticate the users [19]. Authors evaluated their scheme on 310 participants on 60k passcode entries and achieved an Equal Error Rate (EER) of 7.17% on PINs and 6.09% on Android lock patterns.

Kumar et al. [14] presents a motion-based user authentication solution for smartwatches. The authors proposed four variants of continuous user authentication based on user's arm movements while walking. The design incorporated smartwatch's accelerometer and gyroscope sensor data, individually as first and second variants, and then, applied feature- and score-level fusion as the third and fourth variant. The system was tested under three different environments, i.e., intra-session (40 users dataset), inter-session (40 users dataset), and inter-phase (12 users dataset) using four classifiers, namely, k nearest neighbors (k-NN) with Euclidean distance, Logistic Regression, Multilayer Perceptrons, and Random Forest, resulting in a total of sixteen authentication mechanisms. They achieved mean dynamic false accept rate (DFAR) of 0% and dynamic false reject rate (DFRR) of 0% for all of the twelve authentication mechanisms in the intra-session environment. In the inter-session environment, k-NN performed best with mean DFAR of 2.2% and DFRR of 4.2%, for a feature level fusion-based design. Whereas, in the inter-phase environment, the DFAR and DFRR increased to 15.03% and 14.62% respectively for the same feature level fusion-based design with the k-NN classifier.

We consider these motion assisted behavioral-biometric-based studies [20–22] and [24] very relevant to our work. In [20] the authors propose finger-snapping as behavioral modality for user authentication on smartwatches. This scheme also profiles users' arm movements by collecting sensory readings from built-in accelerometer and gyroscope sensors while the user performs the finger-snapping gesture. They reported TAR is 82.34% at an FAR of 34.25% on 15 training samples, by using the Multilayer perceptron classifier (MLP). The study [22] proposes hand-punch behavior as a behavioral modality for smartwatch user authentication. Using one-class SVM as a classifiers on hand-punch gesture data (profiled using accelerometer) of 20 users (with 25 samples from each user), they reported an accuracy of 95.45%. Similarly, in [21] the authors propose smartwatch-worn in-air-finger-writing as behavioral modality for user authentication. By using an MLP 1-class MLP as classifiers, the authors achieved a TAR of 80.52% at 21.65% FAR on 15 training samples. In [24], authors propose to gyroscope-powered in-the-air signing gesture to authenticate the users of smartwatch. Using collected dataset (only gyroscope readings) of 11 volunteers and Dynamic Time Warping (DTW) as classifier, authors achieved 90.1% accuracy.

2.2 Biometric-Based Access Control

The proposals for using physical biometric-based smart access using fingerprint [25], face [26], iris [27] already exist. The study [25] presents a fingerprint-based access control system that exploits simple fingerprint minutiae points (arch, loop, whorl) as features and reports an accuracy of 95%. Similarly, the approach presented in [26] uses face recognition for access control. They implemented their system based on monitoring the eye and mouth state and achieved an over-all accuracy of 98.3%. All these systems, besides their vulnerability to attacks, require explicit user action, hence they lack usability. Additionally, users raised serious privacy concerns in sharing their traits for their verification.

Behavioral biometrics is a less explored area. In [28] the authors present "Smarthandle", which exploits users' hand-movement while they rotate the door handle to unlock the door. By adding an IMU to the door handle, they profile the users based on the user's hand-movements in X, Y, and Z dimensions. By using a Linear Discriminant Classifier (LDC) in an n-class settings, on the data collected from 11 users, the authors report a TAR of 87.27% at an FAR of 1.39%.

The proposed approach, namely CLAPAUTH, is different from the previously described authentication solutions in the following ways: (i) it leverages a novel hand-clapping action that is easy to perform, (ii) the data collection is fully unobtrusive making it suitable for user authentication design, (iii) it has a higher accuracy by using very few training samples (only 9 training samples), (iv) may support a large number of users and (v) it is here evaluated for securing physical access control to a facility. Moreover, our solution could be utilized to transform a smartwatch into a master-key to authenticate or authorize a user to all other connected devices or to access a facility.

3   Approach

The proposed approach is based on the idea of utilizing the arm micro-movements captured while performing clapping as a behavioral biometric modality. The flowchart of our proposed approach is illustrated in Fig. 3. We use n-class classifiers (in Matching box) to authenticate the wearer to access the security facility. It is worth noting that the classification (matching) is done on the server for access control of the facility.

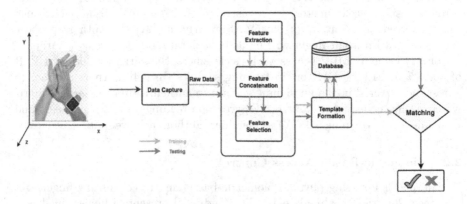

Fig. 3. Block diagram of our approach

CLAPAUTH exploits arms' micro-movements generated from the clapping gesture. The approach starts with the generation of raw data when the user claps. CLAPAUTH captures these movements for the entire period of clapping action and extracts the statistical features from the collected tuples, i.e., (X, Y, and Z dimensions of Accelerometer and gyroscope sensors (as shown in Fig. 3). The dataset we used for this study contains 91 statistical features, i.e., mean, standard deviation, etc., for each sensor. We append the features extracted from the gyroscope sensor at the end of accelerometer sensor features to form a final feature vector of 182 features. Then, this feature vector is transmitted to the centralized server where it is fed to the feature selection module to fetch the most useful (predictive) feature subset for user profiling. The selected feature subset is stored as a template in the servers' database for using it to match the query sample, in order to accept or reject the user.

4   Experimental Validation

4.1   Dataset

The sensory readings corresponding to the clapping gesture are obtained from a publicly available multi-activity dataset [29]. The "WISDM Smartphone and Smartwatch Activity and Biometrics Dataset" was collected by 51 participants[3]. Each participant was asked to perform 18 activities, such as walking, jogging, sitting, standing, or clapping, while wearing a smartwatch in their dominant hand and a smartphone in their pocket. All these activities are labeled from A to S and the processed data (in terms of features) is stored as Attribute-Relation File Format (ARFF) files. In general, the sensory data corresponding to these activities was collected using accelerometer and gyroscope sensors of the smartphones and smartwatches. The type of smartwatch used in the study was an LG G Watch running Android Wear 1.5. The sample rate of data collection was fixed to 20 Hz (50 ms). Since we are interested only in smartwatch sensory readings associated with the clapping gesture, we downloaded and used only the ARFF files labeled with "R" as activity. These ARFF files contain 18 observations for each user, but, for 4 users there are 45 observations.

4.2   Features

The "WISDM Smartphone and Smartwatch Activity and Biometrics Dataset" uses the features depicted in Fig. 4. The first row "ACTIVITY" contains the code of the performed activity, i.e., the code A, B, C, refer to the walking, Jogging, and stairs activities, respectively. Clapping activity is coded with letter R. The sensor data features start from row 2 of Fig. 4. More specifically, the first 30 features are the distribution of values over the X, Y and Z axes (shown in 2nd, 3rd, and 4th rows). Authors called this a binned distribution. For each of the three axes, i.e., X, Y, and Z, they computed the range of values (max-min),

---

[3] However, there are 50 ARFF files (ARFF file for class 1614 is missing) so, we used the available data of 50 users.

divided this range into 10 equal-sized bins, and recorded the fraction of values in each bin. The reader is referred to [29] for better understanding these features content. We exploited all the features of the accelerometer and gyroscope sensors in this study.

Attribute Name	Attribute Type or Values
ACTIVITY	{A,B,C,D,E,F,G,H,I,J,K,L,M,O,P,Q,R,S}
X{0-9}	numeric
Y{0-9}	numeric
Z{0-9}	numeric
{X,Y,Z}AVG	numeric
{X,Y,Z}PEAK	numeric
{X,Y,Z}ABSOLDEV	numeric
{X,Y,Z}STANDDEV	numeric
{X,Y,Z}VAR*	numeric
XMFCC{0-12}*	numeric
YMFCC{0-12}*	numeric
ZMFCC{0-12}*	numeric
{XY, XZ, YZ}COS*	numeric
{XY, XZ, YZ}COR*	numeric
RESULTANT	numeric
class*	{16XX}

Fig. 4. Layout of ARFF headers file [29]

4.3   Feature Fusion

In [30] the authors describe the levels at which collected data could be fused in a biometric system: sensor level; feature; match score; rank and decision level. Data fusion as early as possible is the preferred choice, however, fusion at the sensory level does not typically yield good accuracy because of the presence of noise during the data collection. Conversely, fusion at feature level provides higher accuracy because here the feature representation contains more relevant and accurate information. Therefore, we preferred this latter approach to extract from sensor data the maximum amount of relevant information. The fusion (or concatenation) of 91 available features from the original sensors' signals, determines a new feature vector of 182 features; we call it the feature vector for clap behavior.

4.4   Classifier Selection

We have considered a few simple, yet effective state-of-the-art machine learning classifiers. For our n-class classification task (accessing the secure facility scenario), we relied on Weka [31] - an open-source GUI-based toolbox. In this case we have chosen MLP-based ANN, Random Forest (RF) and IBK as n-class classifiers. We chose these classifiers because of their simplicity, lightweightedness, and effectiveness, as it was shown in similar researches [11,20]. We used these classifiers along with their default settings. Better performances are likely to be attainable with a proper optimizations of the models' hyperparameters. We leave this investigation as future work.

4.5   Feature Selection

Feature selection or variable subset selection is the process of selecting the most predictive feature subset from the original feature set. This step is performed for three reasons. Firstly, this is important for discarding non-informative features. Secondly, feature selection can decrease the computation cost of the full authentication operation, since, processing smaller feature vectors requires less computation as compared to the original feature vectors. Finally, a smaller feature vector is expected to reduce the complexity of the model and can result in a higher generalization capability.

We relied on the CfsSubsetEval (CSE)[4] algorithm to find best feature subset for our task. CSE Evaluates the value of a subset of features by considering the individual predictive ability of each feature along with the degree of redundancy between them [32]. This algorithm applies Greedy Stepwise search in forward direction and evaluates every subset. The best feature subset (with highest accuracy) is returned as the recommended subset. In our case the algorithm returns a 44-feature long vector, with validation accuracy of 93.7%, for our analysis. It is worth mentioning that we use only the training set for feature selection. Later using these feature sets, we evaluated the classifier's testing performance (Table 1).

Table 1. List of selected CSE features

Position	Features					
1–6	Ac_X1	Ac_X9	Ac_X20	Ac_X21	Ac_X26	Ac_XAVG
7–12	Ac_YAVG	Ac_ZAVG	Ac_ZPEAK	Ac_XYCOS	Ac_XZCOS	Ac_YZCOS
13–18	Gy_XYCOS	Gy_XZCOS	Gy_YZCOS	Gy_X0	Gy_X2	Gy_X3
19–24	Gy_X5	Gy_X6	Gy_X10	Gy_X11	Gy_X23	Gy_X24
25–30	Gy_X22	Gy_X25	Gy_X27	Gy_X29	Gy_XAVG	Gy_YAVG
31–36	Gy_ZAVG	Gy_XPEAK	Gy_YPEAK	Gy_ZPEAK	Gy_XABSOLDEV	Gy_XMFCC0
37–42	Gy_YMFCC0	Gy_ZMFCC13	Gy_XYCOS	Gy_XZCOS	Gy_YZCOS .	Gy_XYCOR
43–44	Gy_XZCOR	Gy_RESULTANT	-	-	-	-

4.6   Experimental Settings

We divide, for each user, the dataset into 3 parts: we use 50% of the samples (9, in total) for training the classifiers. Then, we use 20% (5) of the samples for validation and the remaining 30% (5) samples for testing. For the preliminary analysis, i.e., feature selection, we use the validation samples for testing the classifiers and to obtain the validation accuracy. The test set remains unseen by the classifier and used only to obtain the test accuracy to quantify the classifier's performance.

---

[4] https://weka.sourceforge.io/doc.dev/weka/attributeSelection/CfsSubsetEval.html.

4.7   Performance Evaluation

In this work, we use the following measures to assess the system performance:

- **True Acceptance Rate (TAR)**: The rate of correct classification of legitimate attempts.
- **False Acceptance Rate (FAR)**: The rate of incorrect classification of adversarial attempts.
- **False Rejection Rate (FRR)**: The rate of incorrect classification of legitimate attempts.
- **True Rejection Rate (TRR)**: The rate of correct classification of adversarial attempts.
- **Accuracy**: It is the ratio of correct classification to all the classification attempts.
- **Receiver Operating Characteristics (ROC)**: It is a graphical plot between False Accept Rate (on x-axis) and True Accept Rate (on y-axis) used to depict the classification ability of a classifier over the different thresholds. The curve starts from coordinates (0,0) and ends at (1,1). The curve closer to coordinates (0,1) shows higher quality.

4.8   Experimental Results

To compare the authentication performance of different classifiers, we use 9 samples for training, 4 for validation, and 5 for testing. The outcome for the intra-user testing samples (training and testing on the samples of the same user) is either true accept or false reject. Similarly, for inter-user (training on the samples of one user and testing the other users' samples) testing samples, the outcome is either false accept or true reject. These results are added to the results and average results (for all 50 users) are reported. We show the evaluation results in term of TAR, FAR, and Accuracy. We do not report FRR and TRR because they can be easily derived as FRR $= 1 - TAR$, and $TRR = 1 - FAR$.

In Table 2, we summarize the obtained results for the chosen classifiers, when all the available features are used, i.e., before applying any feature selection algorithm. We are able to obtain an accuracy of 86.0%, 89.3%, and 90.7% for RF, ANN, and KNN, respectively. These results are already quite good, as only very few (only 9) samples are used for training. The obtained results clearly indicate that clapping gestures generate significantly different arm-movement signatures that could be effectively used for designing a robust authentication mechanism.

Figure 5 shows the results of the considered classifiers when features are appropriately selected. The chosen classifiers trained on the CSE selected features, yielded the results shown in Fig. 5. It is evident that KNN outperformed other classifiers by attaining a maximum TAR of 93.3% at an FAR of just 0.22%. It has an accuracy of 96.54% and outperforms its counterparts by a significant margin. The obtained results prove the effectiveness of selected features.

Table 2. Classifiers accuracy (%) by using all the features (averaged over 50 users)

	n-class classification		
Classifiers	RF	ANN	KNN
Accuracy	86.0	89.3	90.7

We present the ROC curve of the best performing classifier - KNN, in Fig. 6. The blue and red lines indicate the performance of KNN classifier on full and CSE selected features, respectively, using varying thresholds. It is notable that this classifier performed better on CSE selected features.

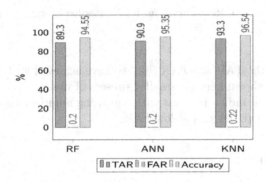

Fig. 5. Obtained results on selected features on Test set (averaged over 50 users)

The performance of the n-class classifier may depend on the number of users that are distinguished. Hence, in order to check if CLAPAUTH is scalable in the number of users, we evaluate the classifier performance for an increasing number of users, from 10 to 40 (50 users results are those already shown). Since we have at our disposal a data set of 50 users, we generate smaller sets of users by discarding some of the available ones and repeat the training and test procedure, which was used before on 50 users, on these smaller sets of users. Actually, since the performance of the system may depend on the particular subset of users that we choose, we repeat the experiment 10 times, for each considered number of users. Hence, for instance, in order to assess the system performance when 20 users are considered we random sample 20 users from the available 50 users, 10 times, and perform the train and test procedure on these 10 samples of 20 users' data. A similar computation was performed with samples of 10, 30 and 40 users.

The results of this analysis, only for the KNN classifier (the other classifiers have similar behaviour), are shown in Table 3. Here, for each number of users ranging from 10 to 40, we show TAR, FAR and Accuracy obtained in each one of the 10 samples of users' sets, and then we show in the last two rows the average results and the standard deviation. It is evident from this table that TAR, FAR, and accuracy remain quite stable across the different sizes of users

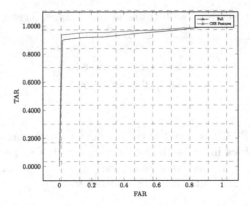

Fig. 6. The comparison of ROC curves for KNN classifier on full and selected features

subsets. Actually the TAR and FAR that we have achieved for 50 users are even better than those shown here for smaller subsets of users.

This gives a clear indication that with a growing number of users CLAPAUTH could still ensure high TARs and low FARs.

5   Discussion

Smartwatches are the most personal devices worn on the arm. Due to the wide adoption of smartwatches in IoT infrastructures, they could be transformed into master-keys to authenticate or authorize users to gain access to secure facilities.

This work focuses on the exploitation of clapping gestures to authenticate the wearer. We present a friction less, user-friendly, scalable and secure user authentication scheme to authenticate the wearer hence helping servers in avoiding trespassing and ensuring secure access to the secure facility.

This work exploits simple supervised classifiers, i.e., KNN, ANN, RF. It is worth-mentioning that we applied these classifiers in default settings, however, the accuracy could be further improved by optimizing these classifiers. We leave this investigation as future work.

KNN outperform its counterparts and achieves 93.3%, at an FAR 0.22% respectively. It should be noted that the classifiers are trained on few samples: just 9, and in their default settings. We are sure that by increasing the number of training samples, adding additional effective features, and optimizing the classifier's parameters, the accuracy of CLAPAUTH could further be improved. We leave this investigation as future work.

As the work exploits the clapping gesture, every one is familiar of, we believe that CLAPAUTH could enjoy wide user acceptance and would not get affected with ageing.

CLAPAUTH is a unimodal system - because it exploits just the one modality, i.e., arm-movement captured while clapping. Multimodal systems have shown to

Table 3. KNN results (%) on different subset sizes of users

Sr.#	10 Users			20 Users			30 Users			40 Users		
	TAR	FAR	Acc	TAR	FAR	Acc	TAR	FAR	Acc	TAR	FAR	Acc
1	87.8	1.4	93.2	93.9	0.3	96.8	93.0	0.2	96.4	91.1	0.2	95.45
2	97.8	0.2	98.8	89.4	0.6	95.8	91.5	0.2	95.65	92.2	0.2	96
3	96.7	0.3	98.2	92.2	0.4	95.9	91.9	0.3	95.8	91.1	0.2	95.45
4	91.1	0.9	95.1	91.7	0.4	95.65	87.8	0.4	93.7	91.9	0.2	95.85
5	91.1	0.9	95.1	92.2	0.4	95.9	93.0	0.2	96.4	91.7	0.2	95.75
6	98.9	0.1	99.4	90.0	0.6	94.7	93.3	0.2	96.55	91.7	0.2	95.75
7	96.7	0.3	98.2	92.8	0.3	96.25	89.3	0.3	94.5	88.6	0.3	95.7
8	94.4	0.6	96.9	94.4	0.2	97.1	91.1	0.3	95.4	91.6	0.2	95.65
9	95.6	0.5	97.55	92.8	0.4	96.2	91.9	0.2	95.8	88.1	0.3	93.9
10	91.1	0.9	95.1	92.8	0.4	95.74	90.7	0.3	95.2	92.5	0.2	96.15
Avg	94.12	0.61	96.75	92.43	0.40	96.0	91.35	0.27	95.54	91.05	0.22	95.56
Std	3.64	0.40	2.02	1.20	0.124	0.657	1.737	0.067	0.89	1.22	0.042	0.624

be more accurate and more secure than their unimodal counterparts. However, by combining multiple modalities, the developed system could become unobtrusive. CLAPAUTH could be extremely useful in such a case: it could use the electromyographic sensory information [33] collected unobtrusively, as a second factor and use it for decision making. We leave this investigation for future work.

CLAPAUTH has however some limitations. Firstly, the user is required to use both hands for performing clapping action, which might not be acceptable to some of the users. Secondly, performing clapping action in public creates noise and may not be suitable in some scenarios, i.e., in a meeting. Finally, our results are still drawn from a limited number of users, i.e., 50 (most of them were students), that could not be considered representatives of the entire population of a real system. However, our scalability analysis has shown that increasing the number of user should not pose a significant problem to the proposed approach.

6 Conclusion and Future Work

In this work, we exploit clapping as a behavioral modality to perform identity verification to securing access to a secure facility. Our study on the clapping gestures of 50 users demonstrated that CLAPAUTH is accurate (up to 96.54% accuracy), user-friendly, and scalable. This implies that we could consider clapping gestures to design an accurate and frictionless authentication mechanism. Moreover, by considering more factors, e.g., electromyography, electrocardiography, etc., we can design and develop a more robust multimodal authentication scheme.

The reported accuracy in terms of TAR, FAR and accuracy is achieved by using the chosen classifiers in default settings. As future work, we plan to investigate if by optimizing the classifiers one can further improve accuracy. Additionally, we plan to check the effectiveness of CLAPAUTH in bi/multi modal setting.

We are in the process of implementing a proof-of-the-concept Android application based on the findings of this work. Then we plan to conduct unsupervised in-the-wild experiments to validate the effectiveness of CLAPAUTH. We plan to extend this work by reporting obtained results in terms of use of resources (power processing and memory usage), robustness to attacks (random, mimic, and engineered), and user acceptance using Software Usability Scale[5](SUS).

References

1. Tavčar, J., Horvath, I.: A review of the principles of designing smart cyber-physical systems for run-time adaptation: learned lessons and open issues. IEEE Trans. Syst. Man Cybern. **49**(1), 145–158 (2018)
2. Krašovec, A., Pellarini, D., Geneiatakis, D., Baldini, G., Pejović, V.: Not quite yourself today: behaviour-based continuous authentication in IoT environments. Proc. ACM Interact. Mob. Wearable Ubiquit. Technol. **4**(4), 1–29 (2020)
3. Smart door locks. http://www.yalelock.it/en/yale/yale-italy/smart-living/smart-door-locks/. Accessed 22 Apr 2022
4. Ho, G., Leung, D., Mishra, P., Hosseini, A., Song, D., Wagner, D.: Smart locks: lessons for securing commodity internet of things devices. In: Proceedings of the 11th ACM on Asia Conference on Computer and Communications Security, pp. 461–472. ACM (2016)
5. Katsini, C., Belk, M., Fidas, C., Avouris, N., Samaras, G.: Security and usability in knowledge-based user authentication: a review. In: Proceedings of the 20th Pan-Hellenic Conference on Informatics, pp. 1–6 (2016)
6. Ometov, A., Petrov, V., Bezzateev, S., Andreev, S., Koucheryavy, Y., Gerla, M.: Challenges of multi-factor authentication for securing advanced IoT applications. IEEE Netw. **33**(2), 82–88 (2019)
7. Yobico: 2020 state of password and authentication security behaviors report. https://pages.yubico.com/2020-password-and-authentication-report. Accessed 22 Apr 2022
8. Buriro, A.: Behavioral biometrics for smartphone user authentication. University of Trento, Italy (2017)
9. Li, L., Zhao, X., Xue, G.: Unobservable re-authentication for smartphones. In: NDSS, vol. 56, pp. 57–59 (2013)
10. Zhang, H., Patel, V.M., Fathy, M., Chellappa, R.: Touch gesture-based active user authentication using dictionaries. In: 2015 IEEE Winter Conference on Applications of Computer Vision, pp. 207–214. IEEE (2015)
11. Buriro, A., Crispo, B., Del Frari, F., Wrona, K.: Touchstroke: smartphone user authentication based on touch-typing biometrics. In: Murino, V., Puppo, E., Sona, D., Cristani, M., Sansone, C. (eds.) ICIAP 2015. LNCS, vol. 9281, pp. 27–34. Springer, Cham (2015). https://doi.org/10.1007/978-3-319-23222-5_4
12. Buriro, A., Gupta, S., Yautsiukhin, A., Crispo, B.: Risk-driven behavioral biometric-based one-shot-cum-continuous user authentication scheme. J. Signal Process. Syst. **93**, 989–1006 (2021)

---

[5] https://measuringu.com/sus/.

13. Primo, A., Phoha, V.V., Kumar, R., Serwadda, A.: Context-aware active authentication using smartphone accelerometer measurements. In: Proceedings of the IEEE Conference on Computer Vision and Pattern Recognition Workshops, pp. 98–105. Springer, Heidelberg (2014)
14. Kumar, R., Phoha, V.V., Raina, R.: Authenticating users through their arm movement patterns, arXiv preprint arXiv:1603.02211 (2016)
15. Nguyen, T., Memon, N.: Tap-based user authentication for smartwatches. Comput. Secur. **78**, 174–186 (2018)
16. Nguyen, T., Sae-Bae, N., Memon, N.: DRAW-A-PIN: authentication using finger-drawn PIN on touch devices. Comput. Secur. **66**, 115–128 (2017)
17. Shang, J., Wu, J.: A usable authentication system using wrist-worn photoplethysmography sensors on smartwatches. In: 2019 IEEE Conference on Communications and Network Security (CNS), pp. 1–9. IEEE (2019)
18. Lewis, A., Li, Y., Xie, M.: Real time motion-based authentication for smartwatch. In: 2016 IEEE Conference on Communications and Network Security (CNS), pp. 380–381. IEEE (2016)
19. Lu, C.X., Du, B., Kan, X., Wen, H., Markham, A., Trigoni, N.: VeriNet: user verification on smartwatches via behavior biometrics. In: Proceedings of the 1st ACM Workshop on Mobile Crowdsensing Systems and Applications, pp. 68–73 (2017)
20. Buriro, A., Crispo, B., Eskandri, M., Gupta, S., Mahboob, A., Van Acker, R.: SNAPAUTH: a gesture-based unobtrusive smartwatch user authentication scheme. In: Saracino, A., Mori, P. (eds.) ETAA 2018. LNCS, vol. 11263, pp. 30–37. Springer, Cham (2018). https://doi.org/10.1007/978-3-030-04372-8_3
21. Buriro, A., Van Acker, R., Crispo, B., Mahboob, A.: Airsign: a gesture-based smartwatch user authentication. In: Proceedings of the 2018 International Carnahan Conference on Security Technology (ICCST), pp. 1–5. IEEE (2018)
22. Liang, G.-C., Xu, X.-Y., Yu, J.-D.: User-authentication on wearable devices based on punch gesture biometrics. In: ITM Web of Conferences, vol. 11, p. 01003. EDP Sciences (2017)
23. Yu, X., Zhou, Z., Xu, M., You, X., Li, X.-Y.: Thumbup: identification and authentication by smartwatch using simple hand gestures. In: 2020 IEEE International Conference on Pervasive Computing and Communications (PerCom), pp. 1–10. IEEE Computer Society (2020)
24. Huang, C., Yang, Z., Chen, H., Zhang, Q.: Signing in the air W/O constraints: robust gesture-based authentication for wrist wearables. In: IEEE Global Communications Conference (Globecom-2017), pp. 1–6. IEEE (2017)
25. Baidya, J., Saha, T., Moyashir, R., Palit, R.: Design and implementation of a fingerprint based lock system for shared access. In: 2017 IEEE 7th Annual Computing and Communication Workshop and Conference (CCWC), pp. 1–6. IEEE (2017)
26. Shi, W., Li, J., Ding, Y., Zhou, K.: Research on intelligent access control system based on interactive face liveness detection and machine vision. In: IOP Conference Series: Materials Science and Engineering, vol. 563, no. 5, p. 052094. IOP Publishing (2019)
27. Yu, L., Li, K., Zheng, J.: Application design of the iris recognition technology in the access control management system. In: IOP Conference Series: Materials Science and Engineering, vol. 719, no. 1, p. 012040. IOP Publishing (2020)
28. Gupta, S., Buriro, A., Crispo, B.: Smarthandle: a novel behavioral biometric-based authentication scheme for smart lock systems. In: Proceedings of the 2019 3rd International Conference on Biometric Engineering and Applications, pp. 15–22. ACM (2020)

29. Weiss, G.M.: Wisdm smartphone and smartwatch activity and biometrics dataset. In: UCI Machine Learning Repository: WISDM Smartphone and Smartwatch Activity and Biometrics Dataset Data Set, vol. 7, pp. 133190–133202 (2019)

30. Jain, A.K., Flynn, P., Ross, A.A.: Handbook of Biometrics. Springer, New York (2007). https://doi.org/10.1007/978-0-387-71041-9

31. Hall, M., Frank, E., Holmes, G., Pfahringer, B., Reutemann, P., Witten, I.H.: The WEKA data mining software: an update. ACM SIGKDD Explor. Newslett. 11(1), 10–18 (2009)

32. Hall, M.: Correlation-based feature subset selection for machine learning. University of Waikato, New Zealand (1998)

33. Raurale, S.A., McAllister, J., Del Rincón, J.M.: EMG biometric systems based on different wrist-hand movements. IEEE Access 9, 12256–12266 (2021)

User Authentication on Headset-Like Devices by Bioacoustic Signals

Dmytro Progonov[1,2]([envelope]) [ORCID], Heorhii Naumenko[1] [ORCID], Oleksandra Sokol[1] [ORCID], and Viacheslav Derkach[1] [ORCID]

[1] Samsung R&D Institute Ukraine, Samsung Electronics LLC, Kyiv, Ukraine
{d.progonov,h.naumenko,o.sokol,v.derkach}@samsung.com
[2] Igor Sikorsky Kyiv Polytechnic Institute, Kyiv, Ukraine

Abstract. Reliable and transparent user authentication on sensor-rich devices, such as wearables, is a topical task today. Of special interest are methods based on bioacoustic signals processing, such as on-body active and passive acoustic sensing. These methods are attractive due to the relatively small aging effect of the captured bioacoustic signals and low battery consumption. This makes them promising candidates for on-device user authentication.

Most recent researches in bioacoustic user authentication are aimed at active acoustic sensing. Practical usage of such methods requires adding of an additional electro acoustic transducer to wearables which is inappropriate for already commercialized devices. Methods of passive acoustic sensing allow for overcoming these limitations by capturing bioacoustic signals produced during person's movements, for example wrist rotations. However, practical application of these methods requires usage of microphones with high sensitivity for capturing of weak acoustic signals. To overcome this limitation we suggest to perform passive sensing near the place with multiple joints, such as cervical vertebrae.

The results of performance analysis proved effectiveness of proposed solutions, namely decreasing of False Rejection Rate (FRR) errors up to ten times in comparison with state-of-the-art solutions while preserving low False Acceptance Rate (FAR) values. Achieved values FAR = 0.12% and FAR = 3.00% for proposed solution conforms to the requirements for Secondary Tier of Android OS Tiered Authentication Model that makes the solution an attractive candidate for user authentication on the next-generation wearable devices.

Keywords: Wearable devices · User authentication · Bioacoustic

1 Introduction

Key drivers of mobile gadgets market in the recent years are smartwatches and earbuds [6,9]. These devices allow for easy tracking of persons health-related parameters, such as heartbeats, oxygenation level, and sleep duration. Also mobile gadgets became essential for interaction with connected devices such as

A. Saracino and P. Mori (Eds.): ETAA 2022, LNCS 13782, pp. 31–47, 2023.
https://doi.org/10.1007/978-3-031-25467-3_3

smartphones and TVs. Despite rich functionality, adoption of wearable devices for new scenarios, such as sensitive data processing, is limited [6]. This is caused by concerns about possible privacy issues, such as disclosure of personal health data.

To overcome these limitations, methods for user authentication based on biometrics (like gait, voice, heartbeat signals) and behavior (motions patterns, usage patterns) data were proposed. These methods leverage built-in sensors for wearable devices while preserving a relatively low computational complexity. Especially promising are those based on processing of bioacoustic signals caused by friction of neck bones near the joints. Uniqueness of such signals for each person and slow degradation of signal parameters due to aging make bioacoustic an attractive alternative for user authentication [11,13,19].

Proposed methods for user authentication by bioacoustic signals can be divided into active and passive ones. The former are aimed at producing of probe acoustic signals and estimate parameters of reflected signal. The latter ones use off-the-shelf equipment for gathering acoustic signals caused by bones frictions [19]. Despite wide range of proposed methods for active bioacoustic sensing, the necessity to use special measurement equipment limits practical application of such methods in commercial wearable devices.

The methods for passive sensing require advanced signal processing methods for extraction of robust features from gathered mixture of weak (low magnitude) bioacoustic signal and ambient noise. Therefore, the majority of such methods are aimed at increasing signal-to-noise ratio by placing microphones as close to a joint as possible. This limits the application of such methods for some types of wearables like VR-headsets, headphones and earbuds where the applicability of bioacoustic authentication is not deeply studied.

This paper is aimed at filling this gap by development of fast and accurate user authentication by passive acoustic sensing for headset-like devices. The main contribution of the paper may be summarized as follows:

1. To the best of our knowledge, this is the first research of bioacoustic signals produced by big skeleton joints, like cervical vertebrae, for user authentication on wearable devices. We checked the case of usage a neckband (neck-based headset) with microphones placed as close as possible to a big joints in the neck. This allows estimating baseline of achievable error level for other types of audio equipment, such as earbuds, VR headsets to name a few.
2. We propose method for accurate non-continuous user authentication by bioacoustic signals gathered by headset devices at the backside of the neck. The method is based on multistage processing of acoustic signals using spectral features and Convolutional Neural Networks (CNN). This reduces values of FAR and FAR to the levels that are applicable for reliable person authentication on modern smartphones [15].
3. The performance evaluation was done for state-of-the-art and proposed methods of user authentication via bioacoustic signals produced by various joints, namely wrist and neck. Considered devices included a smartwatch as a widespread and convenient for user wearable as well as neckband. Estimated

error levels for mentioned cases is of special interest for next generation of user authentication systems on wearable devices.

The rest of this paper is organized as follows. Notations and acronyms are presented in Sects. 2–3. A review of modern solutions for bioacoustic user authentication on wearable devices and purpose of the paper are presented in Sect. 4. Proposed technology for bioacoustic user authentication is described in Sect. 5. Results of performance evaluation are presented in Sect. 6. Section 7 summarizes the paper.

2   Notations

By **boldface** we indicate high-dimensional arrays, matrices, and vectors. Their individual elements will be denoted by the corresponding lower-case letters in *italic*. Calligraphic font is reserved for sets. If nothing extra is specified, then we assume that an element x from a set $\mathcal{X}$ is sampled according to uniform distribution.

Biometric data (a sample) is presented as a vector of real numbers $\mathbf{b} \in \mathbb{R}^n$. Threshold values are denoted as T with the corresponding indices.

3   Acronyms

ATAM Android Tiered Authentication Model
CNN Convolutional Neural Networks
CT Cepstral Transform
DWT Discrete Wavelet Transform
FAR False Acceptance Rate
FFT Fast Fourier Transform
FRR False Rejection Rate
MFCC Mel-frequency Cepstral Coefficient
MLP Multilayer Perceptron
SAR Spoofing Acceptance Rate
STFT Short Time Fourier Transform

4   Literature Review

The key factors for person authentication methods are password (something users known), hardware tokens (something users have), biometric and behavioral data (something that is specific for every individual). The first factor is widely used for granting access to personal computers as well as network services. Token-based authentication is used for corporate services, where reliable person authentication is crucial. Despite low error levels, their practical usage for mobile devices is limited due to the necessity of additional hardware and limitations for password input.

The biometric and behavior-related data can be captured by built-in sensors. For example heartbeat signals – with electrocardiogram sensor, user's gait – by motion sensor. This makes possible to use such a data for continuous authentication, namely liveness tracking by heartbeat signals by Keyble [5], Nymi [8] and BSekur [14] solutions. Also, biometric and behavioral signals are highly dependent on individual physiology which gives low Spoofing Acceptance Rate (SAR). This is crucial for modern operating systems of mobile and wearable devices. For example, requirements for FAR, FRR and SAR values for Android OS is presented in the Table 1.

Table 1. Three classes from Secondary Tier ("What you are") of ATAM [15]. Here IdT is idle timeout period, InA is incorrect attempts number.

Class	Requirements	Capabilities			Constraints	
		Device unlock	Application integration*	Keystroke integration**	Fallback timeout	More constraints
Class 3 (Strong)	SAR: 0%–7% FAR: 1/50K FRR: 10% Secure pipeline	+	+	+	72 h	–
Class 2 (Weak)	SAR: 7%–20% FAR: 1/50K FRR: 10% Secure pipeline	+	+	–	24 h	IdT: 4 h or InA: 3 attempts
Class 1 (Convenience)	SAR: >20% FAR: 1/50K FRR: 10% (In)secure pipeline	+	–	–	24 h	IdT: 4 h or InA: 3 attempts

(*) App integration means exposing an API to apps (e.g., via integration with BiometricPrompt/BiometricManager, androidx.biometric, or FIDO2 APIs)
(**) Keystore integration means integrating Keystore, e.g., to release app auth-bound keys

The novel methods for user authentication on mobile and wearable devices utilize heartbeat signals, such as B-Secur HeartKey [14] and Keyble solution by FlyWallet [3]. However, effective suppression of context or aging related alterations requires using several heartbeats [25]. This also engages computation-intensive models which limits practical application of such approach on resource-constrained wearables.

To overcome these obstacles, behavior-based approaches were proposed, such as BehavioSec [1], BioCatch [2] and Digital Fingerprints [4]. They are based on analysis of behavioral templates that provide reliable user authentication by the cost of computation-intensive processing. Therefore, such solutions rely on coordinated collaborative work of both wearable device (for signal tracking) and a paired smartphone (for data processing and decision making).

The promising approach for biometric-based user authentication on wearables is to leverage bioacoustic signals. These signals are produced by frictions of person's bones during natural body movements that can be tracked with built-in microphones. The domain of bioacoustic takes special interest today for applications related to early detection of lungs [13] and bones [21] issues, hand gesture recognition by wrist's bones frictions [10], touch interaction in virtual reality [23], person identification [11], to name a few.

Close connection of bioacoustic signals with persons physiology (for example, joints parameters) and slow degradation due to aging effect make such signals promising candidates for user authentication. Bioacoustic signals based methods can be divided into active and passive acoustic sensing [26]. The former methods are based on analysis of audio signals transmitted through person body area (for example, a wrist) with usage of additional electro acoustic transducer [19,21, 31]. Parameters of these signals, like magnitude and shape, strictly dependent on bones parameters that makes such methods attractive candidates for user authentication even in presence of external acoustic noises.

Modern approaches to processing of bioacoustic signals captured with active sensing actively use spectral transformations as well as CNN. The former approach is based on Fast Fourier Transform (FFT) [26], Cepstral Transform (CT) [31], mel-spectrograms and Mel-frequency Cepstral Coefficient (MFCC) [21], VELODY features [20] and statistics for spectral coefficients [19]. The second group is based on feature extraction from raw signals with CNN [26] as well as hybrid networks [28]. This allows to improve the accuracy of user authentication by captured bioacoustic signals even in presence of external noise.

The methods for passive sensing are aimed at capturing weak acoustic signals produced by bones frictions. This requires usage of special measurement equipment, namely microphones with high sensitivity, for gathering of such signals. Also, preserving high signal-to-noise ratio for captured signals requires usage of wearable only in places with low ambient noise level that may be impractical.

Therefore, researchers are concentrated on development of advanced processing methods for detection, extraction and analyzing low-magnitude bioacoustic signals. The majority of such studies are focused on the case, where wearables are put above or close to the wrist [21,26,31] that allows to increase the magnitude of captured signals. Still, bioacoustic signals produced by other joints in human body did not draw much attention. We proposed to analyze signals produced in the neck's backside during head motions. Several joints (vertebrae) in this area can produce individual "cracks" during movements that increase the total magnitude of bioacoustic signals. Such signals can be captured by built-in microphones of modern headsets and in-ear headphones due to bones conduction effect. Processing of such bioacoustic signals remains a non-trivial task due to low signal magnitude level and requires special processing methods. These methods are computationally-intensive which makes them inappropriate for resource-limited wearable devices.

Thus, development of accurate and computationally-efficient methods for user authentication by such signals is required. The paper is devoted to the development of low-complexity methods for person authentication by bioacoustic signals produced by cervical vertebrae joints. Performance analysis is done for state-of-the-art and proposed methods of processing of bioacoustic signals generated by wrist and neck motions.

5   Proposed Solution

User authentication by bioacoustic is based on analysis of acoustic signals produced by frictions of bones during movements. The magnitude and shape of produced sounds highly depend on negligible variations of bones shapes as well as joints (cartilages) parameters for each person that makes it possible both user identification and authentication.

For usability purposes, of special interest are bioacoustic signals captured by wearables located near wrists, such as smartwatches and fitness trackers. This makes it possible to reliably collect bioacoustic signals caused by hand motions, but magnitude of signals remains relatively low. This is caused by features of wrist physiology, namely connections of ensemble of bones with relatively small size [22].

Therefore, relocation of microphones to bigger cartilages allows to increase the magnitude of captured signals and to simplify theirs processing. The joints located in the neck are good candidates: there are seven stacked bones called cervical vertebrae (Fig. 1).

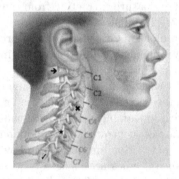

Fig. 1. Positions of bones (vertebrae C1–C7) and cartilages in the human neck area. According to [7].

The head motions lead to friction of vertebrae known as "neck crepitus" (bone-on-bone grinding)—adjacent vertebral bones can start rubbing against each other, which may cause a grinding noise. This produces sound waves whose parameters depend on motions magnitude, angles between vertebrae as well as physiological parameters of connected bones. Note that head motions exert high pressure on relatively small cervical vertebrae that leads to increasing of bones grinding [22]. Therefore, acoustic signals produced by vertebrae during head motions have much larger magnitude in comparison with wrist joints. Also, these signals can be captured with microphones embedded into modern headset devices, like virtual reality headset, headphones and earbuds. This makes cervical vertebrae be an attractive candidate for capturing bioacoustic signals related to user authentication tasks.

Despite increasing of bioacoustic signals energy for cervical vertebrae in comparison with wrist joints, the magnitude of such signals remains relatively low. Therefore, for feasibility checking we modified a headset included into the accessory set of modern smartphones. It includes substitution of built-in microphone with high sensitivity electret condenser microphone, and adding of low-noise pre-amplifier. The general view of modified headset is presented in Fig. 2.

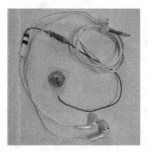

(a) The general view of used headset

(b) The low-noise pre-amplifier

(c) The integrated high-sensitivity electret microphone

Fig. 2. Modified headset for capturing bioacoustic signals caused by neck bones grinding

The captured signal of head motions consists of a mixture of low magnitude acoustic signals caused by bones grinding and ambient noises (for example, friction of clothes and hairs with skin). Due to low energy of mentioned acoustic signals, the electret microphone with high sensitivity is used (Fig. 2c). The low-noise pre-amplifier (Fig. 2b) is added to increase the magnitude of captured bioacoustic signal while preserving low level of ambient noises.

The modified headset (Fig. 2) was used for capturing bioacoustic signals from three volunteers for various head motions patterns. The tests signals were obtained for two cases: for our custom hand-made headset and for Galaxy Watch3 smartwatch. The former case allows us to compare sounds "neck crepitus", while the latter ones represent sounds of bone-on-bone grinding near the wrist area. The examples of captured signals are presented in Fig. 3. Due to differences in magnitude and duration of captured signals, they are pre-processed to have equal duration and unit energy.

Note that shape and time locations of peaks of captured signals are specific for each person (Fig. 3). Also, these parameters preserve if motion pattern changes. This proves the hypothesis of the dependency of bioacoustic signals on small differences in bones and joints structure.

The shape of signals captured on the backside of the neck includes several pulses with relatively high duration (Fig. 3a–b). This is caused by friction of huge areas of cervical vertebrae bones. To the contrary, impulses for bioacoustic

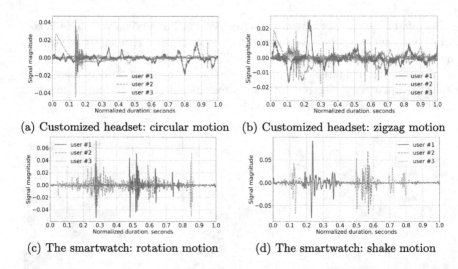

(a) Customized headset: circular motion   (b) Customized headset: zigzag motion

(c) The smartwatch: rotation motion   (d) The smartwatch: shake motion

Fig. 3. Examples of bioacoustic signals captured by customized headset and Galaxy Watch3 smartwatch with built-in microphone

signals captured with smartwatch are much shorter (Fig. 3c–d). This is due to friction of several bones with much smaller area at the wrist joints.

Modern approaches for user authentication by bioacoustic signals are based on applying spectral transformations, namely FFT [26] and CT [31]. This is caused by two reasons: easy physical interpretation of obtained spectrum (which simplifies noise and outliers removal), and the ability to obtain fixed length spectrum for signals with varying duration. Still, feature selection from raw spectrum for person verification remains a non-trivial task that is typically solved by ad-hoc empirical methods.

The state-of-the-art methods for user authentication by bioacoustic signals produced by neck's bones frictions were proposed by Sim [26] and Watanabe [31]. The first method is based on applying CNN for feature extraction from Fourier spectrum of signals. The structure of proposed CNN is shown at Fig. 4.

The proposed neural network (Fig. 4) consists of two parts: feature extraction by a set of convolutions and full-connection (dense) layers, and further classification by the last layer. The input data for the network is Fourier spectrum for captured signal up to 3 kHz with the step 10 Hz (totally 300 harmonics):

$$\mathbf{X}_k = \sum_{n=0}^{N-1} x_n \times e^{-i2\pi kn/N}, k \in [0; N-1],$$

where x_n—samples of captured signal of length N samples; k—index of harmonic in estimated Fourier spectrum.

The model proposed by Watanabe et al. is based on applying of CT for separation of informative signal from ambient noises [31]:

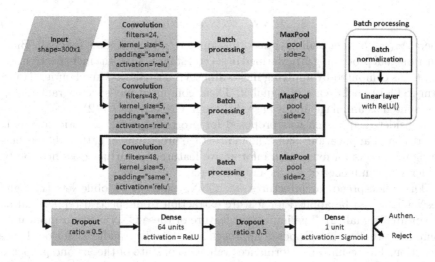

Fig. 4. Structure of CNN proposed by Sim et al. [26] for person authentication by bioacoustic signals.

$$\mathcal{C} = \left| \mathcal{F}^{-1} \left\{ \log \left(|\mathcal{F}\{f(t)\}|^2 \right) \right\} \right|^2,$$

where $\mathcal{C}$—calculated cepstrum; $\mathcal{F}, \mathcal{F}^{-1}$—direct and inverse Fourier transforms respectively; $f(t)$—input signal as function of time. Estimated ceptrum is used as a feature vector for further processing with ensemble classifier.

The considered approaches are based on using spectral transformation that produces short (compressed) representation of bioacoustic signals. Nevertheless, applied FFT and CT use harmonic basis (sine and cosine functions) that are inappropriate for decomposition of pulse-like signals due to Gibbs effect [24]. This leads to spreading of energy for such signals over a wide frequency range that complicates noise suppression.

Alternative approach is based on applying signal processing pipelines from audio processing domain, namely the use of MFCC [19] and mel-spectrogram [21]. This makes it possible to apply advanced methods for noise suppression of widespread types of distortions, such as microphone sensor noise and reverberation to name a few. Still, these methods are aimed at detection of high magnitude acoustic signals that may negatively impact low-energy bioacoustic signals processing.

We propose to apply special methods of weak acoustic signal processing to overcome the described limitations of state-of-the-art methods. Our proposed technology is based on two-stage processing of gathered acoustic signal $\mathbf{x} = (x_1, \ldots, x_N)$ with usage of mel-spectrogram $\mathbf{f}_{MS}$ and CNN:

$$\mathbf{f}_{MS} = \mathcal{M} \left(\sum_{n=-\infty}^{+\infty} \mathbf{x}_n \omega(n-m) e^{-j\omega n} \right), \tag{1}$$

$$\mathbf{f}_{CNN} = \mathcal{F}_{CNN}(\mathbf{f}_{MS}), \tag{2}$$

where $\mathcal{M}(\cdot)$—be mel-scaling transformation; $\omega(\cdot)$—be a window function. Bioacoustic signal processing is performed in several stages. First, the mel-spectrogram $\mathbf{f}_{MS}$ (1) is computed by applying mel-scaling $\mathcal{M}(\cdot)$ to Short Time Fourier Transform (STFT) coefficients of signal $\mathbf{x}$. Then, computed mel-spectrogram $\mathbf{f}_{MS}$ is represented as an image and is passed through CNN $\mathcal{F}_{CNN}(\cdot)$ (2).

Considered approach was proposed for processing weak acoustic signals in sonar-related applications [30]. The multi-stage processing of gathered bioacoustic signals allows for extraction informative features for further classification by reducing the influence of noises and interference.

The widespread architectures of CNN, such as MobileNet [17] and ResNet [16], can be applied for feature extraction from spectral representation of captured signal (2). The important feature of these CNN is low computation complexity that makes proposed approach an attractive candidate for on-device execution. The results of performance evaluation of state-of-the-art and proposed methods are shown in the next section.

6   Experiments

Performance evaluation of considered methods for user authentication by bioacoustic signals was performed for cases of passive acoustic sensing near the wrist and at the backside of a neck. The former case is related to the modern researches of user authentication with wearables, such as commercial smartwatches, while the latter one corresponds to the case of headset-like devices usage for user verification, such as fitness headsets.

Let us note absence of publicly available open datasets for passive acoustic sensing on both smartwatches and headset-like devices. Thus, the in-house dataset of bioacoustic signals was prepared with usage of Galaxy Watch3 smartwatch and modified headset (Fig. 2). The gathered dataset includes signals for seven presumably healthy persons (two males and five females) captured in a room with low level of background (ambient) noise, such as traffic noise, alarms, extraneous speech, electrical noise from air conditioning, power supplies, etc. The volunteers were still sitting during signals collection to minimize influence of impulse noises caused by friction of clothes and hairs with skins. The performance evaluation did not include analysis of long-term changes of bioacoustic signals due to COVID-19. Thus, we would like to cover cases of injures and diseases, muscle tensions changes (training tiredness), habits alterations in future works.

Signals gathering was performed by placing our customized headset on the back of a neck, below the hairline, and wearing of Galaxy Watch3 at convenient place near the wrist. The following motions templates were considered during the dataset preparation:

- Cervical vertebrae grinding sounds:
  - Circular motions—a head is rotated clockwise with maximum magnitude;
  - ZigZag motions—a head is rotated to left shoulder, then from left to right shoulders, and finally from right shoulder to the normal position;
- Wrist grinding sounds:
  - Rotation motion—a wrist is rotated clockwise with maximum magnitude of rotation;
  - Shake motions—a hand and wrist is moved up and down with forceful and jerky movements;
  - Grip motion—a hand takes and keeps a firm hold of an object placed in front of a volunteer at the table.

Captured signals were re-sampled to standard sampling rate 44.1 kHz for audio processing. Then, signals were split into tiles (intervals) for each mentioned motion templates. Prepared signals were passed through low-pass filters (cutoff frequency was 8 kHz), and then filtered by median (reduce impulse noise, 15 samples window size) and Wiener (reduce additive noise, 31 samples window size) filters to remove external noises. Finally, signals were normalized by energy and re-sampled to 1 second duration.

Features extraction from gathered signals were performed by the following methods:

- *Spectral features*—are based on applying to captured signals the widespread spectral transformations, like FFT and Discrete Wavelet Transform (DWT). The one-level DWT with Haar wavelet and the corresponding scaling function was used. The magnitude spectrum for FFT and approximation coefficients for DWT were used as features.
- *Acoustic-specific features*—are related to widespread methods of statistical features extraction from audio signals. The case of mel-spectrogram and MFCC with sampling frequency of 16 (kHz) was considered. The mel-spectrogram (1) was estimated by usage of STFT with Blackman-Harris window. The obtained spectra were used as features.
- *Proposed features*—the mel-spectrograms were computed with STFT with Blackman-Harris window. Then, obtained spectrograms were rescaled to 8-bits range (grayscale image) and passed through a CNN. The output from penultimate layer of a CNN was used as features. For feature extraction according to proposed method, we considered CNN that are widely used in on-device applications: MobileNet [17], ResNet [16], Inception [27], Xception [12], DenseNet [18], NasNetLarge [32] and EfficientNet-B1 [29].

Also, proposed solution was compared with state-of-the-art methods proposed by Sim et al. [26] and Watanabe et al. [31]. The former method is based on applying the CNN to the Fourier spectrum of captured signal, while the latter one uses CT for spectral features extraction.

The two types of classifier were used due to extensive size of extracted feature (up to 11, 136 features for mel-spectrogram)—ensemble classifier, namely Random Forest, and Multilayer Perceptron (MLP). The former classifier allows for effective suppression of curse of dimensionality (insufficiency of the number of collected signals in comparison with their size). The latter one relates to the widespread case of applying neural networks for both features extraction and classification. The Random Forest classifier was additionally adjusted to minimize error level by varying the number of base learners from 100 to 1,000 with step 100.

Considered methods were evaluated by the standard cross-validation with splitting of dataset into train (70%) and test (30%) subsets ten times. The FAR and FRR were used as metrics for methods comparison. These indices were estimated by averaging results for each person from collected dataset. To reduce negative impact of low fraction of target user's samples in comparison with other user, the class weighting procedure was applied.

To evaluate proposed approach, we estimated FAR and FRR by usage of spectral, acoustic-specific an proposed features for bioacoustic signals captured by wearable and headset. Obtained results are presented in the Table 2.

Due to features of Sim et al. method [26], the estimated values of FAR and FRR are presented for the MLP classifier (Table 2). Note that the estimated values of FAR and FRR are much higher for Random Forest classifier in comparison of MLP. This can be explained by presence of cross-dependencies between feature's elements, for example, by presence of harmonics of a base tone or by narrow spectrum of signals components. These dependencies can be eliminated by applying bagging technique in ensemble classifier. This effect is negligible for MLP due to processing of the whole feature vector in layer-wise fashion.

The use of spectral and acoustic-specific features allows to minimize error level for the case of Random Forest (Table 2). Applying of MLP leads to additional decrease of FAR and FRR values up to two times. Minimal error values for MLP are achieved by proposed approach which proves its effectiveness in comparison with the existing state-of-the-art methods.

The MLP helps to decreasing error levels considerably in comparison with Random Forest based classifier (Table 2), as it was for the case of smartwatch usage (Table 2). Note that obtained values of FAR and FRR for proposed approach are close to the requirements for Secondary Tier for authentication systems of Android OS (Table 1). This makes proposed approach to be a promising candidate for on-device user authentication.

Moreover, applying the novel CNN architectures including EfficientNet or NasNet may be improve results even further. Comparative analysis of FAR and FRR values for proposed solution for various CNN and bioacoustic signals is presented in the Table 3.

Indeed, modern EfficientNet network allows for decreasing half total error rate in comparison with considered earlier ResNet network up to three times for all motion patterns (Table 3). Therefore, practical application of authentication systems based on processing bioacoustic signals produced by wrist motions has considerable limitations. This is caused by insufficient accuracy for state-of-the-art solutions as well as significant increase of FAR values (up to 2.5%) for

Table 2. Estimated FAR (P_α) and FRR (P_β) values by applying of spectral and acoustic features for bioacoustic signal processing. Note that Sim et al. method is based on usage of ad-hoc multilayer perceptron classifier. The minimal and maximum values of half total error rate (half sum of FAR and FRR) for each motion pattern are marked with green and red colors respectively.

| | Galaxy Watch3 smartwatch | | | | | | Modified headset | | | |
| | Rotation motion | | Shake motion | | Grip motion | | Circular motion | | ZigZag motion | |
	P_α, %	P_β, %	P_α, %	P_β, %	P_α, %	P_β, %	P_α, %	P_β, %	P_α, %	P_β, %
Random Forest classifier										
Sim et al. method	—	—	—	—	—	—	—	—	—	—
Watanabe et al. method	0.00	100.00	0.00	100.00	0.00	100.00	0.00	100.00	0.00	96.80
Fourier transform	1.70	64.56	0.88	82.36	1.29	76.88	0.94	39.80	3.88	42.40
DWT	0.04	99.86	0.60	93.58	0.14	99.39	0.24	99.60	0.00	98.80
Mel-spectro-gram	1.08	74.48	2.01	54.08	1.34	86.31	3.53	40.00	1.88	27.80
MFCC	0.92	72.99	0.77	58.20	0.82	80.99	0.35	25.00	0.00	18.60
MobileNet	0.31	75.41	0.89	61.81	0.35	88.57	0.12	31.80	0.59	24.00
ResNet-50	0.12	75.07	0.14	64.25	0.11	89.37	0.12	37.20	0.71	35.40
Multilayer Perceptron classifier										
Sim et al. method	19.50	32.15	38.28	29.91	33.56	22.50	9.98	8.40	8.91	15.20
Watanabe et al. method	6.93	90.59	5.29	83.77	6.45	85.14	12.73	83.20	14.19	72.80
Fourier transform	2.72	45.58	2.72	71.87	3.16	64.30	4.24	21.40	3.04	35.60
DWT	30.17	66.00	28.87	63.95	26.26	66.12	31.73	72.40	28.66	56.80
Mel-spectro-gram	17.66	81.43	12.64	87.00	16.63	83.01	13.29	84.00	16.71	78.00
MFCC	2.57	74.87	2.10	67.67	2.79	78.95	2.12	45.60	3.66	43.00
MobileNet	2.20	34.94	1.11	29.62	3.48	57.62	0.82	14.60	0.65	13.20
ResNet-50	1.80	43.68	1.30	27.54	1.27	52.90	0.12	9.00	0.71	16.20

proposed method. These limitations can be attributed to the decreasing magnitude of bioacoustic signals due to permanent repetition of motion patterns during signals gathering.

Note considerable decrease of error values for considered case in comparison with the previous one (Table 3)—the FRR values are decreased up to 30% for Random Forest classifier, and up to 12 times for MLP while preserving low values of FAR $(FAR \leq 0.2\%)$.

This can be explained by differences between magnitude of bioacoustic signals captured by smartwatch and neckband. The larger magnitude of signal for neckband simplifies detection and extraction of informative features in comparison with case of smartwatch usage. Therefore, we may conclude that proposed

Table 3. Estimated FAR (P_α) and FRR (P_β) values by applying of proposed method for bioacoustic signal processing. The minimal and maximum values of half total error rate (half sum of FAR and FRR) for each motion pattern are marked with green and red colors respectively.

| | Galaxy Watch3 smartwatch | | | | | | Modified headset | | | |
| | Rotation motion | | Shake motion | | Grip motion | | Circular motion | | ZigZag motion | |
	P_α, %	P_β, %	P_α, %	P_β, %	P_α, %	P_β, %	P_α, %	P_β, %	P_α, %	P_β, %
Random Forest classifier										
DenseNet-121	0.11	69.88	0.46	48.37	0.15	79.90	0.12	36.80	0.24	22.20
DenseNet-169	0.35	67.49	0.61	51.07	0.34	80.66	0.24	32.40	0.24	16.40
DenseNet-201	0.35	63.63	0.68	48.60	0.20	79.89	0.12	24.20	0.12	18.20
EfficientNet-B1	0.11	66.36	0.39	47.30	0.38	75.33	0.12	25.20	0.71	29.40
NasNet-Large	0.41	70.42	0.43	57.10	0.19	84.19	0.12	33.20	0.00	18.60
ResNet-101	0.34	76.49	0.18	64.32	0.00	88.32	0.00	40.40	0.47	38.80
ResNet-152	0.04	83.85	0.14	66.81	0.00	88.72	0.00	45.80	0.12	34.80
Xception	0.15	75.92	0.21	61.49	0.47	87.33	0.24	42.40	0.35	18.00
Inception	0.26	77.34	0.14	65.54	0.24	85.47	0.35	36.00	0.00	37.60
Multilayer Perceptron classifier										
DenseNet-121	2.07	38.75	1.62	24.72	2.48	47.65	0.47	16.40	0.35	10.00
DenseNet-169	1.82	36.01	1.69	30.61	2.11	53.90	1.41	8.80	0.47	13.40
DenseNet-201	1.11	33.93	1.72	26.21	2.23	48.19	0.71	10.00	0.12	3.00
EfficientNet-B1	2.50	24.10	1.11	20.55	1.81	40.94	0.24	3.00	0.59	3.80
NasNet-Large	2.36	34.22	1.86	27.81	2.66	53.03	0.59	11.20	0.82	3.60
ResNet-101	2.32	40.92	1.37	25.93	1.93	58.22	0.59	16.00	1.53	13.40
ResNet-152	0.93	29.14	1.11	27.92	1.69	58.47	0.24	9.20	0.12	14.80
Xception	2.41	47.00	0.89	28.24	3.74	54.37	0.34	21.00	0.12	6.60
Inception	1.82	37.44	1.40	35.13	2.99	47.96	1.06	13.00	1.02	8.80

solution allows for considerable improvement of FAR and FRR values in comparison with state-of-the-art solutions while preserving a relatively low computation complexity.

7   Conclusion

Wearable devices, such as fitness trackers, smartwatches and headsets, are widely used these days. They naturally blend into our daily routine by providing convenience features in a natural non-intrusive way. Typically, these devices are equipped with rich set of sensors including embedded microphones reliably placed close to the signal source. This makes it possible to use them for reliable on-body detection, identification and user authentication applications, such as pay-by-watch, or using as 2nd authentication factor for various applications on companion mobile phone.

In this paper we made performance evaluation of modern methods for user authentication by bioacoustic signals gathered with off-the-shelf smartwatches.

The results showed their limitation for practical usage in user authentication tasks due to high error level (up to 2% FAR and 83% FRR). It can be explained by high influence of external noises (such as friction of device and skin). To overcome these limitations we proposed to capture bioacoustic signals near the place of several bones joints, and to apply methods from sonar-related technologies. The former gives an opportunity to increase the magnitude of captured bioacoustic signals by involving several vertebrates and cartilages into motions. The latter one allows extraction the weak informative signal from a mixture with noises. This makes possible effective suppression of the negative impact of external noises while preserving informative features for further classification.

Estimated values of FAR and FRR proved the effectiveness of our proposed solution, namely the decrease of FRR errors up to ten times while preserving low FAR values. Let us note that these results were obtained by usage of neckband (headset located at the neck), where built-in microphone was placed as close as possible to the cervical vertebrae. Also, obtained results related to the case of processing bioacoustic signals that did not altered with long-term alterations, such as injures and diseases, muscle tensions (training tiredness), habits changes to name a few. Therefore, of special interest is applicability of proposed solution for other types of audio equipment, such as wireless headsets, earbuds and bone-conductivity based earphones. We plan to make more research for these devices as well as tracking long-term changes of bioacoustic signals in the future.

References

1. BehavioSec: Supercharge your Multi-factor authentication. https://www.behaviosec.com/. Accessed 24 Mar 2022
2. BioCatch: Every Swipe Tells a Story. https://www.biocatch.com/. Accessed 24 Mar 2022
3. CES 2021: Wearable Device with Biometric Authentication. https://www.eetimes.eu/ces-2021-wearable-device-with-biometric-authentication/. Accessed 02 Mar 2021
4. Digital Fingerprints: T's Not What You Do It's The Way You Do It. https://fingerprints.digital/. Accessed 24 Mar 2022
5. Flywallet: Keyble Overview. https://www.flywalletpay.com/en/. Accessed 02 Mar 2021
6. Fortune Business Insights: Mobile Analytics Market Size, Share & Industry Analysis. https://www.fortunebusinessinsights.com/mobile-analytics-market-104824. Accessed 29 Mar 2022
7. NeuroRehab Coach: Anatomy of the Neck. https://www.neurorehabcoach.com/neck-pain. Accessed 24 Mar 2022
8. Nymi: Product Overview. https://www.nymi.com/product. Accessed 04 Dec 2020
9. The Insight Partners: Mobile Analytics Market Forecast to 2028. https://www.theinsightpartners.com/reports/mobile-analytics-market. Accessed 29 Mar 2022
10. Asakura, T., Iida, S.: Hand gesture recognition by using bioacoustic responses. Acoust. Sci. Technol. **41**, 521–524 (2020). https://doi.org/10.1250/ast.41.521. https://www.jstage.jst.go.jp/article/ast/41/2/41_E1949/_pdf/-char/en

11. Chauhan, J., Hu, Y., Seneviratne, S., Misra, A., Seneviratne, A., Lee, Y.: Breath-print: breathing acoustics-based user authentication. In: MobiSys 2017: Proceedings of the 15th Annual International Conference on Mobile Systems, Applications, and Services. ACM (2017). https://doi.org/10.1145/3081333.3081355

12. Chollet, F.: Xception: Deep Learning with Depthwise Separable Convolutions. https://doi.org/10.48550/arXiv.1610.02357. https://arxiv.org/abs/1610.02357. Accessed 28 Mar 2022

13. Errico, C., et al.: Ultrafast ultrasound localization microscopy for deep super-resolution vascular imaging. Nature **527**, 499–502 (2015). https://doi.org/10.1038/nature16066. https://www.nature.com/articles/nature16066#citeas

14. Goodwin, A.: B-Secur HeartKey tech unlocks your car with unique rhythm of your heartbeat. https://www.cnet.com/roadshow/news/b-secur-ekg-heartkey-tech-unlocks-car-with-heartbeat/. Accessed 04 Dec 2020

15. Google: Lockscreen and authentication improvements in android 11 (2020). https://android-developers.googleblog.com/2020/09/lockscreen-and-authentication.html

16. He, K., Zhang, X., Ren, S., Sun, J.: Deep Residual Learning for Image Recognition. https://doi.org/10.48550/arXiv.1512.03385. https://arxiv.org/abs/1512.03385. Accessed 28 Mar 2022

17. Howard, A.G., et al.: MobileNets: Efficient Convolutional Neural Networks for Mobile Vision Applications. https://doi.org/10.48550/arXiv.1704.04861. https://arxiv.org/abs/1704.04861. Accessed 28 Mar 2022

18. Huang, G., Liu, Z., van der Maaten, L., Weinberger, K.Q.: Densely Connected Convolutional Networks. https://doi.org/10.48550/arXiv.1608.06993. https://arxiv.org/abs/1608.06993. Accessed 28 Mar 2022

19. Lee, S., Choi, W., Lee, D.H.: Usable user authentication on a smartwatch using vibration. In: ACM SIGSAC Conference on Computer and Communications Security. ACM (2021)

20. Li, J., Fawaz, K., Kim, Y.: Velody: nonlinear vibration challenge-response for resilient user authentication. In: SIGSAC Conference on Computer and Communications Security. ACM (2019). https://doi.org/10.1145/3319535.3354242

21. Lu, F.Y., Husske, L., Roesler, A.: WristConduct: biometric user authentication using bone conduction at the wrist. In: Proceedings of ACM Measurement and Analysis of Computing Systems. ACM (2022)

22. Marieb, E., Hoehn, K.: Human Anatomy & Physiology, 11th edn. Pearson, London (2018)

23. Meier, M., Streli, P., Fender, A., Holz, C.: Tapid: rapid touch interaction in virtual reality using wearable sensing. In: Virtual Reality and 3D User Interfaces (VR). IEEE (2021). https://doi.org/10.1109/VR50410.2021.00076

24. Oppenheim, A.V., Schafer, R.W.: Discrete-Time Signal Processing. Pearson, London (2009)

25. Progonov, D., Sokol, O.: Heartbeat-based authentication on smartwatches in various usage contexts. In: Saracino, A., Mori, P. (eds.) ETAA 2021. LNCS, vol. 13136, pp. 33–49. Springer, Cham (2021). https://doi.org/10.1007/978-3-030-93747-8_3

26. Sim, J.Y., Noh, H.W., Goo, W., Kim, N., Chae, S.H., Ahn, C.G.: Identity recognition based on bioacoustics of human body. Trans. Cybern. **51**, 2761–2772 (2021). https://doi.org/10.1109/TCYB.2019.2941281. https://ieeexplore.ieee.org/document/8859636

27. Szegedy, C., Vanhoucke, V., Ioffe, S., Shlens, J., Wojna, Z.: Rethinking the Inception Architecture for Computer Vision. https://doi.org/10.48550/arXiv.1512.00567. https://arxiv.org/abs/1512.00567. Accessed 28 Mar 2022

28. Takahashi, N., Goswam, N., Mitsufuji, Y.: MMDenseLSTM: an efficient combination of convolutional and recurrent neural networks for audio source separation. In: Saracino, A., Mori, P. (eds.) 16th International Workshop on Acoustic Signal Enhancement (IWAENC), Tokyo. IEEE (2018). https://doi.org/10.1109/IWAENC.2018.8521383

29. Tan, M., Le, Q.V.: EfficientNet: Rethinking Model Scaling for Convolutional Neural Networks. https://doi.org/10.48550/arXiv.1905.11946. https://arxiv.org/abs/1905.11946. Accessed 28 Mar 2022

30. Tanveer, M.H., Zhu, H., Ahmed, W., Thomas, A., Imran, B.M., Salman, M.: Mel-spectrogram and deep CNN based representation learning from bio-sonar implementation on UAVs. In: International Conference on Computer, Control and Robotics. IEEE (2021). https://doi.org/10.1109/ICCCR49711

31. Watanabe, H., Kakizawa, H., Sugimoto, M.: User authentication method using active acoustic sensing. J. Inf. Process. **29**, 370–379 (2021). https://doi.org/10.2197/ipsjjip.29.370. https://www.jstage.jst.go.jp/article/ipsjjip/29/0/29_370/_pdf/-char/ja

32. Zoph, B., Vasudevan, V., Shlens, J., Le, Q.V.: Learning Transferable Architectures for Scalable Image Recognition. https://doi.org/10.48550/arXiv.1707.07012. https://arxiv.org/abs/1707.07012. Accessed 28 Mar 2022

The Measurable Environment as Nonintrusive Authentication Factor on the Example of WiFi Beacon Frames

Philipp Jakubeit[1]([✉]), Andreas Peter[1,2], and Maarten van Steen[1]

[1] University of Twente, Drienerlolaan 5, 7500 AE Enschede, The Netherlands
{p.jakubeit,a.peter,m.r.vansteen}@utwente.nl
[2] University of Oldenburg, Ammerländer Heerstraße 114-118,
26129 Oldenburg, Germany
andreas.peter@uol.de

Abstract. We explore a method to fingerprint a location in terms of its measurable environment to create an authentication factor that is nonintrusive in the sense that a user is not required to engage in the authentication process actively. Exemplary, we describe the measurable environment by beacon frames from the WiFi access points in the user's proximity. To use the measurable environment for authentication, measurements must be sufficiently discriminating between locations and similar at the same location. An authentication factor built from the measurable environment allows us to describe a user's location in terms of measurable signals. Describing a location in terms of its measurable signals implies that we do not require an actual geographical mapping of the user's location; comparing the measured signals is sufficient to create a location-based authentication factor. Only recognizing an earlier observed environment distinguishes our approach from other location-based authentication factors. We elaborate on using signals in the user's environment in the background without user involvement to create a privacy-preserving but nonintrusive authentication factor suitable for integration into existing multi-factor authentication schemes.

1 Introduction

Multi-factor authentication schemes are the de facto standard when it comes to user authentication. *Authentication* is the 'provision of assurance that a claimed characteristic of an entity is correct' [11]. Authentication factors are conceptually grouped according to the characteristic claimed: knowledge, possession, biometry, and location [2]. The standard in multi-factor authentication schemes in 2022 is two-factor authentication. When authenticating to a particular service, the first factor is typically based on a username-password combination. Only the legitimate user is assumed to know this combination (knowledge-based authentication claim). The second authentication factor is usually a token sent to the user's registered device (SMS, Authenticator app) to strengthen the assurance

© Springer Nature Switzerland AG 2023
A. Saracino and P. Mori (Eds.): ETAA 2022, LNCS 13782, pp. 48–69, 2023.
https://doi.org/10.1007/978-3-031-25467-3_4

that the user is who he claims to be. The user must retype or confirm this token to the service to get authenticated (possession-based authentication claim). We aim to extend this scheme by taking the user's location into account. Extending implies that the knowledge-based and possession-based authentication factors remain parts of the scheme. We add location as a third authentication factor to the two-factor scheme. Location as a claim characteristic might even replace the second factor in certain situations.

The advantage of a location-based authentication claim is that the characteristic claimed does not require the user's active involvement. The location is about the whereabouts of a user, not the user himself. To not require a user to be actively involved in the authentication process is called *nonintrusive authentication* [16]. Nonintrusiveness allows the user to be undisturbed and the service to adjust the remote trust [22] that the user is whom he claims to be. Nonintrusiveness also solves the problem of infrequent authentication [22], the shortcoming that authentication only occurs at the beginning of a session. In other words, using a user's location as an authentication factor allows the service to probe the user for his authentication claim at any time during the session.

The disadvantage of location as an authentication factor is twofold. On the one hand, the claimed characteristic is not of the specific user but the user's environment. On the other hand, a user's location is privacy-sensitive information as it maps the whereabouts of the user when using traditional means to describe the user's location (e.g., GPS or IP subnet ranges).

We asked ourselves how far these disadvantages are necessary for location-based authentication and how we can avoid them. These disadvantages provide us also with an insight into privacy sensitivity. Intuitively, a service only needs to validate a claimed characteristic of the location. Therefore, we do not need to consider where a location is in terms of geographical mapping (like with GPS or IP addresses). We only need to validate the claimed characteristic of the location. To explore this further, we choose the *measurable environment* (ME) as the claimed characteristic of a location.

The ME consists of electromagnetic signals in our surroundings. Appropriate sensors can measure these signals. In the following, we investigate whether it is possible to fingerprint a user's measured environment. A successful fingerprinting scheme of the ME allows us to compare MEs, distinguish different environments and recognize similar environments. For the purpose of authentication, we compare a measured environment of a location to an earlier observed measurement of the location and compute the similarity of measurements.

We envision the ME as an authentication factor to extend the described standard two-factor authentication scheme to a three-factor authentication scheme which assures knowledge, possession, and consistency of the ME. After the username and password prompt, the service can decide to use the second factor and the ME or even replace the second factor with the ME during the login phase. The service checks whether it recognizes the newly observed ME of the user and uses this claim to assure the user's authenticity. Such an authentication factor allows the service to assure consistency of the user's ME, not just during the login time but continuously. The ME as an authentication factor is only limited by the ME's availability, the user's bandwidth, and the time it takes to fingerprint a location in terms of its ME.

We choose WiFi to fingerprint the ME as it is a ubiquitous signal, and the vast majority of devices have sensors to receive WiFi signals. We construct an ambient WiFi fingerprint from beacon frames emitted by WiFi access points (APs) to indicate their presence. We measure these emitted beacon frames for a particular duration at a specific location to construct a fingerprint.

In the remainder of this paper, we discuss how an ME can be fingerprinted and classified before presenting our WiFi instantiation. We continue evaluating the performance of our classification of an ME in terms of WiFi beacon frames. Having a working fingerprinting mechanism, we focus on integrating the WiFi fingerprints into an authentication scheme and discuss the security of authentication based on the ME. We compare our results with results from the literature and close with a discussion, including paths for future works and our conclusions.

2   The Measurable Environment (ME)

We assume the ME as a noisy source, conceptually similar to biometric features of an individual [15] or unique hardware features [7] of devices. We further assume that some ME will be present at most locations. Using a specific sensor, we can pick up a measurement of the ME at a specific location and time. We will position a sensor at certain locations to conduct measurements during specific times. We use these fixed measurements to conduct and evaluate our classification.

2.1   Illustration of the ME

The signals and the sensor must be available for a measured environment to be suitable for fingerprinting. If signals and sensors are available, the ME must have two additional properties to be viable for fingerprinting: measurements of different MEs must be different, and measurements of the same ME must be similar over time. Both need to be evaluated on a per sensor and per signal basis. In Fig. 1, we show three measured environments which we mapped to the two-dimensional space for illustrative purposes only. Figure 1 shows by its visible clusters that measurements of the same ME taken at different times are similar. We also observe that the different locations have no overlap in their measured MEs.

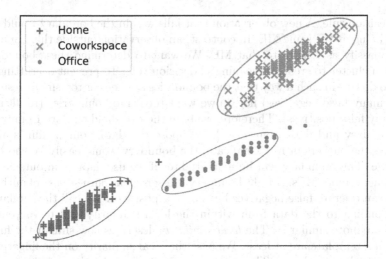

Fig. 1. Illustration of measurements taken at three different MEs: at home, at work, and in a coworking space. Each point represents a fingerprint of a specific ME of one second. The distance between the points describes their similarity. The clusters of points represent a template of an ME, and the boundaries surrounding the clusters represent the threshold of this specific template. If a newly obtained fingerprint falls within the boundaries, we classify the fingerprint as taken at the same ME associated with the template. The figure further shows that the distance between some fingerprints of the ME in the office and the home case fall outside their boundary. These outliers represent false negatives in a classification.

2.2   Fingerprinting the ME

We assume a *sensor* s, which is capable of measuring the environment, taking a *measurement* m. For this work, s is fixed at a specific location. Two measurements m and m' of the same ME are unlikely to be identical because physical-environment data is measured, which is susceptible to interference. To get a more detailed description of the ME, we take multiple measurements of the same ME into account. We build a *fingerprint* $\mathbf{F}$ from a set of measurements by a single sensor s during a time window of t seconds. The associated sensor is denoted as $s(\mathbf{F})$, and the duration of the set of measurements as $t(\mathbf{F})$. To be capable of recognizing a fingerprint, we construct a *template* $\mathbb{F}$ from a set of n fingerprints measured by a single sensor s at the same ME. The associated sensor is denoted as $s(\mathbb{F})$. In Fig. 1 this correlates to taking a cluster of n points as the template.

2.3   Classifying Fingerprints of MEs

When measuring an environment, we want to check if we are dealing with an ME we observed earlier. That means we require a similarity metric and a decision rule to derive whether two fingerprints are sufficiently similar.

In Fig. 1, the distance of one point toward a cluster of points describes their similarity. The elliptic boundary around a cluster of points forms the threshold for a decision rule. A new observation that falls within the boundary would classify as being at the same ME. In contrast, an observation outside this boundary would classify as remote to that ME. We want to determine these boundaries around a cluster to create a meaningful decision rule. To prevent overfitting, we want to do this in such a way that the boundaries are neither too small (resulting in too many false negatives) nor do we want too large boundaries (resulting in too many false positives). Therefore, we base the threshold on data from within the boundary and data from outside. Suppose the data from within is all we have. As the outliers in Fig. 1 indicate, the boundary would easily be chosen as too large. The boundary will be much tighter if we use data from outside, i.e., from other remote MEs. A tight boundary is essential as our use case of authentication can tolerate false negatives but no false positives. We call the similarities corresponding to the data from within the local similarity and to the outside data the remote similarity. The *local similarity* describes how similar the fingerprints of a template are at least. We base the local similarity on the fingerprints of one template we know. The *remote similarity* describes how similar remote fingerprints and the template are. Ideally, we would have access to all possible fingerprints of MEs worldwide that are remote to the template in question. However, getting remote fingerprints of all other MEs is infeasible. Therefore, we approximate the remote similarity by sampling measurements from remote MEs to construct a set of remote fingerprints.

We use our decision rule to decide whether an unlabeled fingerprint is sufficiently similar to a template, based on whether the similarity of a fingerprint and a template is greater or equal to a threshold. Using the local and remote similarity, we compute a threshold per template. In Fig. 1, the threshold correlates to the boundaries around a cluster. Knowing the local similarity of a template allows us to check whether a new, unlabeled fingerprint is sufficiently similar to a template to classify as being at the same ME. Knowing the remote-similarity estimate, we can check whether a new, unlabeled fingerprint is sufficiently dissimilar to classify as being remote to the ME. Combining both, the local and the remote similarity, to the threshold of a template grants us the knowledge that at least every fingerprint observed would be classified correctly. Our decision rule is congruent with a binary classification of the fingerprint. We can phrase it as asking whether the fingerprint belongs to the same ME as the template. If so, we conclude that the ME is identical (i.e., the fingerprint was measured at the template's location). Otherwise, we classify a fingerprint as remote to the ME of the template.

3   Instantiation Using WiFi Beacon Frames

We measure WiFi signals to describe the ME. We consider the availability of the spectrum's signals and the availability of the sensor itself. WiFi is a ubiquitous signal in urban environments, with sensors being ubiquitous in consumer devices. Most WiFi access points (APs) emit a beacon frame signal to indicate their presence. A user measures these beacon frames sent by the APs in his surroundings to conduct a measurement. Measuring the beacon frames does not require a user to connect to a WiFi AP. The user only records WiFi signals in his proximity.

We use the composition of APs to build a fingerprint of a specific ME. In the following, we refer to the WiFi receiver as *sensor s*. It measures the WiFi APs in its proximity. A *measurement m* contains a representation of the beacon-frame features received by the sensor $s(m)$. The number of features of one beacon frame depends on the AP and the sensor. The hardware capabilities determine the sensor's ability to receive beacon frames. The software determines which features of the beacon frames are accessible to the user. We denote an *access point representation (APR)* from a measurement m by $APR(m)$. We build the APR from the features provided by the AP. We distinguish the features between identifying features and capability features. The identifying features of an AP's beacon frame determine the AP uniquely. These are the service set identifier (SSID) and its media access control (MAC) address. However, both data are personally identifiable information (PII). The EU classifies a MAC address belonging to a user even in its hashed form as PII [27]. Because we ask a user to measure his environment, we can not even distinguish whether an AP belongs to the user or not. The SSID is most likely also PII as the SSID might contain names or addresses but also, in the default state, describes the vendor and model of the AP. Another problem with the SSID is that it is potentially volatile since the user can rename it. A WiFi beacon frame also contains capability features. These capability features are not PII as they encode the capabilities of the AP itself. In our case, the maximum bandwidth to use, the security and capability flags, the frequency used, and the mode of the AP. In our evaluations, we base an APR on these capability features to omit the use of PII completely.

If we use the MAC address as APR, the APR becomes unique, and a fingerprint must match a template, assuming that a set of MAC addresses only occurs at one ME (no involvement of spoofing). When using the capability features, the APRs are not unique. However, we show that using only capability features, the sets of APRs from a fingerprint are sufficiently distinguishable for different MEs. Regarding the amount of information of an APR, the MAC address [9] consists of 48 bits, the SSID of 256 bits, and the capability features are dependent on the operating system (OS). We choose the Linux OS in which the specification defines 63 bits [8]. These 63 bits are the maximum entropy possible but will likely not represent the amount of information in real-world measurements. To approximate a more realistic estimate of information per APR, we analyze our data in Sect. 5.2 to derive a lower bound for the observed information. Further, we found that privileged access on Linux (root space) and Windows allow for more capability features, while OSX and mobile operating systems seem more limited in accessing capability features.

Aside from the APR, we focus on the received signal-strength indicator (RSSI), which shows the perceived signal strength of a sensor and is denoted by $RSSI(m)$. The unit of an RSSI value is decibel, often mapped to a percentage. We normalize it such that $RSSI(m) \in [0,1]$. The RSSI is sensor and software dependent, which is no problem as we intend to fingerprint an ME on a per-sensor basis. We expect that including the RSSI value allows us to increase the fraction of relevant instances among the retrieved instances. We plot a measurement in Fig. 2 to illustrate the relationship of the RSSI to its proximity to the sensor while also showing the differences in the APRs.

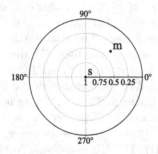

Fig. 2. A measurement m plotted in its polar coordinates. We center the sensor and have a decreasing radial coordinate $r = 1 - RSSI(m)$ being the perceived signal strength from the sensor and an angular coordinate $\varphi(APR(m)) = \frac{APR(m)}{max(APR)} * 2\pi$ being the normalized APR mapped to the unit circle.

3.1 Dataset

Online available datasets of WiFi data are either not clustered according to an ME or do not contain the beacon-frame features we focus on to build the APR. Therefore, we create our own dataset by conducting WiFi measurements, which we published.[1] We use off-the-shelf WiFi receiver hardware in laptops (e.g., [10]) as sensors and conduct our measurements with several such sensors. We keep a sensor at a fixed location for a duration of four hours. We receive $60 * 60 * 4 = 14400$ aggregated fingerprints of $t = 1$ s per ME. We consider twelve MEs recorded by ten different sensors, nine representing a home environment and three representing a work environment. We conducted all measurements at MEs such that there is no physical overlap of the received WiFi APs. Additionally, we consider a thirteenth set of fingerprints, the remote set. In total, we take 187,200 fingerprints of $t = 1$ s of the 12 MEs and the remote set into account.

3.2 Feasibility

We conduct preliminary estimates to assess whether there is a correlation between the observed APs and the ME of a sensor. To estimate the APRs' influence on the ME, we calculate the adjusted mutual information (AMI) [25]. Mutual information (MI) is the amount of information obtained about one random variable by observing another. The definition of the AMI uses H to indicate

---

[1] https://gitlab.com/WiFiFingerprinting/Data.

Shannon entropy [24] and the expected value E. The adjusted mutual information corrects for chance and returns a nonmetrical value. A value close to 0
indicates that there is no correlation. A value of 1 indicates that knowing feature X fully determines the label Y. The authors of [25] state that the larger
the feature-to-label ratio becomes, the more the AMI approaches zero. If the
ratio is larger than 100, they assume an AMI fairly close to zero. Therefore, they
advise using the minimum entropy of X and Y as the normalization function
if the feature-to-label ratio becomes too large. We estimate that an APR has
about 10 bits (see Sect. 5.2), and we know that we have 12 MEs. We compute
the AMI with X being the APRs and Y being random labels assigned to the
specific MEs. We start by considering a single APR. In this case, the ratio of
values of X and the number of labels Y is about 100. Therefore, we define the
AMI to be:

$$AMI(X,Y) = \frac{MI(X,Y) - E\{MI(X,Y)\}}{min(H(X),H(Y)) - E\{MI(X,Y)\}}$$

We are computing the AMI per APR, which results in an AMI of 0.78. We
perceive this value as too low for classification, especially for our application of
authentication. To further measure the impact of APRs on the ME, we computed
the AMI for tuples of APRs. Using tuples for X increases the feature-to-label
ratio by several orders of magnitude, making it even more relevant to choose
the minimum as the normalization function. In the 2-tuple case, we already get
an AMI of 0.95. It gets closer to 1 for each increment in tuple length. For a
4-tuple, we already get an AMI of 0.98. However, the space complexity grows
out of proportion. We observed between 1 and 42 single APRs per fingerprint.
Therefore, we have up to $\binom{42}{k}$ k-tuples to consider.

This space complexity problem is also why classical machine learning
approaches requiring one-hot encoding of categorical values require considerable space complexity during training and a significantly increased load during classification. One-hot encoding would introduce an unnecessary memory
requirement on the device conducting the classification. Therefore, we use a Jaccard similarity-based approach. It does not have this space complexity problem
as there is no training phase except computing the threshold once per template
and our proposed mechanism only uses a list of single APRs with corresponding
RSSI values as the template. We always consider the maximum available APR
combinations by using the Jaccard similarity because we have seen that using
more APRs increases the AMI, which is achievable from a performance point of
view.

3.3   Fingerprinting the ME

We construct a fingerprint $\mathbf{F}$ of the ME in the WiFi instantiation from a set of
measurements of a single sensor s during a time interval of t seconds. We expect
that a fingerprint of a longer duration increased the hit rate. Additional to the
sensor $s(\mathbf{F})$, and the duration $t(\mathbf{F})$, we denote the identified set of APRs as

APR(F). The number of times an AP has been measured during fingerprinting **F** we denote as:

$$|\mathbf{F}; AP| = |\{m \in \mathbf{F}|APR(m) = AP\}|$$

We denote the received signal strength of a measured AP during fingerprinting as $RSSI(\mathbf{F}; AP)$, is defined as the average of the individual measurements:

$$RSSI(\mathbf{F}; AP) = \frac{\sum_{m \in \mathbf{F}, APR(m) = AP} RSSI(m)}{|\mathbf{F}; AP|}$$

The template $\mathbb{F}$ from one ME is represented by a set of n fingerprints received by a single sensor s. Therefore, the template is constructed from $t \times n$ measurements of a single, spatially fixed sensor s. Additional to the sensor $s(\mathbb{F})$ we denote the set of APRs from the template as **APR($\mathbb{F}$)**.

3.4   Similarity of Fingerprints and Templates

The fingerprint **F** and the template $\mathbb{F}$ are sets of APRs with their corresponding RSSI values. To compute their similarity, we apply a standard measurement for set comparison, the Jaccard similarity [12], and create a variant that considers the RSSI value. We choose the Jaccard similarity because it enables us to always consider the maximum available APs while being lightweight in terms of computational and space complexity. We denote the *Jaccard similarity* of a single fingerprint **F** and a template $\mathbb{F}$ by:

$$JS(\mathbf{F}; \mathbb{F}) = \frac{|\mathbf{APR(F)} \cap \mathbf{APR(\mathbb{F})}|}{|\mathbf{APR(F)} \cup \mathbf{APR(\mathbb{F})}|}$$

This version of the Jaccard similarity does not take the RSSI into account. It takes only the APR into account and computes the ratio of APRs present in the fingerprint and APRs present in the template to all APRs present in the fingerprint and the template. Using the JS implies that only the APR determines the similarity of a fingerprint and a template. Figure 3 shows a plot of this.

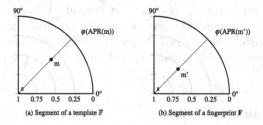

Fig. 3. Two segments of a fingerprint and a template. The template depicts a measurement m and the fingerprint a measurement m'. We assume that $APR(m) = APR(m')$ and that $RSSI(m) \neq RSSI(m')$. When calculating their similarity with $JS(\mathbf{F}; \mathbb{F})$, m' and m are assumed to be equal as it takes only the APR into consideration.

We construct a specific Jaccard similarity that accounts for the requirement that matching APRs have a similar RSSI value. Two RSSI values are similar if they differ at most by a difference $d(\mathbb{F})$. We denote the absolute difference, using $\|$ to denote the absolute value, of the RSSI values of an AP occurring in two fingerprints $\mathbf{F}$ and $\mathbf{F}'$ by:

$$\|\mathbf{F}; \mathbf{F}'; AP\| = \|RSSI(\mathbf{F}'; AP) - RSSI(\mathbf{F}; AP)\|$$

The similarity measure taking the RSSI into account works on a subset of $\mathbf{F}$. This subset is defined such that the RSSI values of a measurement with a matching APR from a fingerprint $\mathbf{F}$ and a template $\mathbb{F}$ differ at most by $d(\mathbb{F})$, for $d(\mathbb{F}) \in [0, 1]$. If $d(\mathbb{F}) = 0$, the RSSI values of a measurement in a fingerprint $\mathbf{F}$ and a template $\mathbb{F}$ have to be equal. The size of $d(\mathbb{F})$ determines how many RSSI values are accepted to be sufficiently similar. Thus, the closer $d(\mathbb{F})$ becomes to 1, the more likely it is that the similarity taking the RSSI value into account is equal to its counterpart that does not take the RSSI value into account. We compute $d(\mathbb{F})$ per template and define it as:

$$d(\mathbb{F}) = max\{\|\mathbf{F}; \mathbf{F}'; AP\| \mid AP \in \mathbf{APR}(\mathbf{F}) \cap \mathbf{APR}(\mathbf{F}'), \mathbf{F}, \mathbf{F}' \in \mathbb{F}, \mathbf{F} \neq \mathbf{F}'\}$$

Choosing $d(\mathbb{F})$ to be a model parameter allows us to cover the difference of the RSSI values measured from the same APR observed in a fingerprint $\mathbf{F}$ and in a template $\mathbb{F}$. We define the subset as:

$$\{\mathbf{F}; \mathbb{F}\} = \{\mathbf{F}' \in \mathbb{F} \mid (\|\mathbf{F}; \mathbf{F}'; AP\| < d(\mathbb{F})) \text{ with } AP \in \mathbf{APR}(\mathbf{F}) \cap \mathbf{APR}(\mathbf{F}')\}$$

Assuming this subset, we can construct the similarity measure, which considers the RSSI value. The *Jaccard similarity with RSSI* of a single fingerprint $\mathbf{F}$ and a template $\mathbb{F}$ is defined as:

$$JSR(\mathbf{F}; \mathbb{F}) = \frac{|\mathbf{APR}(\{\mathbf{F}; \mathbb{F}\})|}{|\mathbf{APR}(\mathbf{F}) \cup \mathbf{APR}(\mathbb{F})|}$$

Whether a measurement with $APR(m)$ in a fingerprint $\mathbf{F}$ and in a template $\mathbb{F}$ is assumed to be the same is dependent on the RSSI value. A measurement m must fulfill two requirements to be an element of the intersection. First, the $APR(m)$ must occur in the fingerprint and the template. Second, the $RSSI(m)$ from the fingerprint and the template must differ at most by the fixed distance $d(\mathbb{F})$. Figure 4 depicts a plot of this.

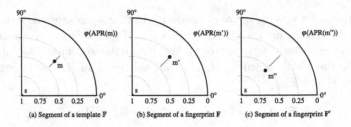

Fig. 4. Three segments of a template ($\mathbb{F}$) with a measurement m and its RSSI difference $d(\mathbb{F}) = 0.1$, and of the fingerprints $\mathbf{F}$ and $\mathbf{F'}$. In a) the measurement is depicted by a dot labeled m and the difference $d(\mathbb{F})$ is depicted by a line with a length of $2d$ (added and subtracted from the $RSSI(m)$ of the measurement in the template). In segment b) the measurement is depicted by m' such that $APR(m') = APR(m)$. It shows an RSSI value inside the boundary (i.e. $RSSI(m') > RSSI(m) - 0.1$). In segment c) the measurement is depicted by m'' such that $APR(m'') = APR(m)$. It shows an RSSI value outside the boundary (i.e. $RSSI(m'') > RSSI(m) + 0.1$).

3.5 Determining the Similarity Threshold

We compute the threshold per template and per similarity measurement $SIM \in \{JS, JSR\}$. The local similarity is the lowest similarity observed between each fingerprint that makes up a particular template and the template itself. This guarantees that all fingerprints used to build the template are more similar than the threshold and implies that a classifier based on this threshold would classify all fingerprints used to build the template correctly. We define it as:

$$local(SIM; \mathbb{F}) = min(\{SIM(\mathbf{F}, \mathbb{F}) \mid \mathbf{F} \in \mathbb{F}\})$$

We also use fingerprints from remote MEs as a reference to determine the threshold. Such a fingerprint $\mathbf{R}$ is built from measurements that are not at the ME of a template. We build a diverse set of fingerprints from these remote fingerprints $\mathbb{R}$. We cap the number of APRs per fingerprint $\mathbf{R}$ at the maximum number of observed APRs in the template to allow for a similarity-based comparison. The remote similarity is the largest similarity observed between each remote fingerprint taken into account and the template itself. This guarantees that all remote fingerprints from $\mathbb{R}$ have a similarity lower than the threshold. Implying that a classifier based on this threshold would classify all remote fingerprints correctly (not belonging to $\mathbb{F}$). We define it as:

$$remote(SIM; \mathbb{F}; \mathbb{R}) = max(\{SIM(\mathbf{R}, \mathbb{F}) \mid \mathbf{R} \in \mathbb{R}\})$$

We compute the **threshold** T by taking the average of the local and the remote similarity, using both balances the threshold by introducing some tolerance. We expect a new fingerprint at the ME with a slightly lower similarity than observed to have a higher similarity than the threshold. We also expect a new remote fingerprint with a slightly higher similarity than the similarities observed to have a lower similarity than the threshold. Choosing the threshold to be the local and remote similarity average prevents the overfitting of the training data used to create the threshold. Given a similarity measure SIM, a template $\mathbb{F}$ and a set of remote fingerprints $\mathbb{R}$ we denote the threshold by:

$$T(SIM; \mathbb{F}; \mathbb{R}) = \frac{(local(SIM; \mathbb{F}), remote(SIM; \mathbb{F}; \mathbb{R}))}{2}$$

3.6 Classifying Fingerprints

The necessary elements to define our decision rule as a classifier are the components and tools for comparison we defined. Our components are: a measurement, the fingerprint, and the template. Our tools for comparison are: the similarities and a template-specific threshold. Our fingerprinting mechanism aims to classify a fingerprint $\mathbf{F}$ by computing its similarity with a template $\mathbb{F}$. If the similarity is larger than the template-specific threshold, we classify the fingerprint as being at the template's ME. Otherwise, we classify the fingerprint as remote to the template's ME. The classifier returns this Boolean decision and we denote it by:

$$C(SIM; \mathbf{F}; \mathbb{F}; \mathbb{R}) = SIM(\mathbf{F}; \mathbb{F}) > T(SIM; \mathbb{F}; \mathbb{R})$$

The classifier C allows us to fingerprint the ME in terms of ubiquitous WiFi beacon frames. It is limited only by the surrounding WiFi APs and the time $t(\mathbf{F})$ required to fingerprint a ME.

4 Performance

We distinguish two models for classification based on the similarity measure used. We either only compare the APRs by applying the JS, or we also consider the RSSI values and apply the JSR. We also vary the time t (in seconds) listened in for a WiFi fingerprint. We started our experiments with $t = 20$ s and increased it incrementally to one minute. Further, we vary the number of WiFi fingerprints n to build a template. We take n to represent a template of the equivalent of 15 min, 30 min, one hour, and two hours (e.g., assuming $t = 20$, the two hours of fingerprint data accumulate to $n = 360$ fingerprints used to build a template). The model parameters are the threshold $T(SIM, \mathbb{F}, \mathbb{R})$ and the tolerated RSSI difference $d(\mathbb{F})$. We compute the RSSI distance $d(\mathbb{F})$ from a template. In our data set, we observe only a slight variation for the values for $d(\mathbb{F})$ per template (at most 0.08), which confirms our expectation that the RSSI increases the uniqueness of measurements.

4.1 Classification

We classify a fingerprint $\mathbf{F}$ based on a template $\mathbb{F}$ and a threshold $T(SIM, \mathbb{F}, \mathbb{R})$. We assume the template to be known for the classification step and derive the threshold from the fingerprints used for building the template and the set of remote fingerprints $\mathbb{R}$. Per ME, we consider fingerprints taken for the total duration of four hours ($t = 14400$). We split the observed fingerprints in half. The latter half, the second two hours, always form the test set. For the training set, we vary the number of fingerprints used in the first half to represent 15 min, 30 min, one hour, and two hours. We compute the similarity of the fingerprint and the template. If the fingerprint's similarity to the template is larger or equal to the threshold, we consider the fingerprint to be measured at the same ME as the template.

To determine the performance of our classifier, we look at its precision and recall. Both are defined in terms of the predicted conditions. The *precision* measures the true positives among all positives predicted. It is defined as: $precision = \frac{TP}{TP+FP}$. The focus is on the false positives. In our context, these translate to remote fingerprints, which classify as being at the ME. The *recall* measures the true positives among all real positives. It is defined as: $recall = \frac{TP}{TP+FN}$. The focus is on the false negatives. In our context, these translate to fingerprints of the ME, which we classify as not being at the ME. The *accuracy* measures correct predictions among the total number of cases examined. It is defined as: $accuracy = \frac{TP+TN}{TP+TN+FP+FN}$. It combines the false positives and the false negatives in one value.

4.2 Validation

We partition our data into two sets: fingerprints of the ME and remote fingerprints. The fingerprints of the ME form the template and the input for computing the local similarity per ME. The remote fingerprints form the input for computing the remote similarity, a limited collage of WiFi fingerprints of various MEs. Both directly influence our threshold T.

We deal with a limited set of remote fingerprints, with different fingerprints from different MEs. To verify the impact of different compositions of fingerprints used to construct the remote similarity, we conduct a Monte Carlo cross-validation (MCCV). Per ME, we randomly shuffle the remote fingerprints before splitting them between the training and the test set. We chose MCCV due to our limited remote fingerprints' set size and our classification mechanism. We deal with an equally partitioned set. Hence, folded cross-validation would not provide a sufficient answer. Even though we deal with a time series, rolling cross-validation is not required for the remote fingerprints. We apply the MCCV v times and choose $v = n$, the training and test sets' sizes. The MCCV allows us to test for v compositions of the remote fingerprint data we consider. We present the precision and recall as our results per MCCV iteration.

4.3 Results

We conduct classifications for all MEs' fingerprints according to the structure described in Sect. 4.1. We start with taking fingerprints of length $t = 20$ s into account and compute a template from $n \in \{45, 90, 180, 360\}$ fingerprints. Our results show that building a template from more fingerprints, a larger n, provides more information about the ME, which is consistent with our expectations.

However, we are aiming for higher precision and recall. The Jaccard similarity taking the RSSI into account produces a much more stable result. We continued with taking fingerprints of length $t = 30$ s into account and compute a template from $n \in \{30, 60, 120, 240\}$ fingerprints. Again the Jaccard similarity taking the RSSI into account produces a much more stable classification result. Still, we are aiming for higher precision and recall. However, we observe a smoothing compared to the $t = 20$ s case. This trend continues and provides near-perfect results when we take fingerprints of length $t = 60$ s into account. We compute a template from $n \in \{15, 30, 60, 120\}$ fingerprints. All choices of n provide promising results. The precision in the case of the JS is lower when most of the time, only a single AP can be measured (e.g., the ME labeled $L8$). For the JS and the JSR, we show the precision per MCCV iteration in Fig. 5. In the case of the JSR, all MEs have a precision greater than 0.98.

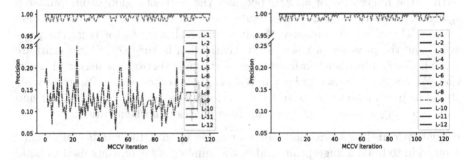

Fig. 5. Precision for the case of JS (left) and JSR (right) with $t = 60$ and $n = 120$, for $v = 120$ MCCV iterations.

The recall in the case of the JS is for all MEs greater than 0.99, except $L8$. It has a recall very close to zero. It would never classify the location $L8$ correctly because it mainly contains only a single AP. For the JSR, all other MEs have a recall greater than 0.99. On the one hand, the recall of ME $L8$ becomes 0.975. On the other hand, the recall of the ME $L5$ has a larger variation. We show the JS's and JSR's recall per MCCV iteration in Fig. 6.

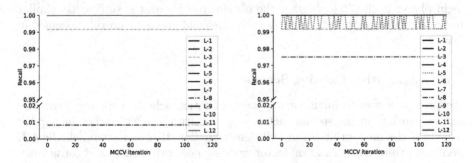

Fig. 6. Recall for the case of JS (left) and JSR (right) with $t = 60$ and $n = 120$, for 120 MCCV iterations.

We observed that choosing a larger n, thus using more fingerprints to build a template, lowers the number of false negatives, which is consistent with our expectations. If we have a more detailed picture of the situation, we can map a new observation more accurately. The consistent performance of the JSR in contrast to the JS confirms our expectations that similar RSSI values allow us to map a newly observed AP with higher precision. By performing better than our AMI estimate (0.98 with only four APs) we also confirm our expectation as we consider all APs. The ME labeled $L8$ even shows that MEs with too few (e.g., one) APRs should not be used.

5   Use Case: Nonintrusive Authentication

We now propose to use the ME as a nonintrusive authentication factor. In this setting, the fingerprint of an ME becomes the authentication claim validated against a template. We focus on extending an existing two-factor authentication scheme. Therefore, the presence of a first authentication factor (e.g., the password) and the presence of a second authentication factor (e.g., SMS token) are a given. To conduct authentication, we distinguish between a user and a service. We assume the user to have a WiFi-capable sensor with software capable of conducting measurements and the service to be capable of registering and authenticating a user. We distinguish three phases of authentication:

Registration: The service and the user agree upon t, the number of seconds listened in to build a fingerprint, and n, the number of fingerprints used to build a template. In the following, the user conducts $n * t$ stationary measurements and combines them to a template $\mathbb{F}$. This template is stored on the service side after successfully authenticating with the previously mentioned first and second factors. The server is further assumed to hold a remote set $\mathbb{R}$.

Login: The user's sensor conducts t stationary measurements and combines them into a fingerprint $\mathbf{F}$. The user then sends this fingerprint $\mathbf{F}$ to the service after being authenticated with the mentioned first and second factors.

Verification: The service has a template of a registered user. To verify the authentication request of a user, the service obtains the fingerprint $\mathbf{F}$ of the login phase. It classifies whether the obtained fingerprint is sufficiently similar to the user's template by computing the threshold and decision rule specified in Sect. 2.3.

5.1   Augmenting Existing Schemes

We present a way to augment any authentication scheme with our ME. The service can invoke the second factor (e.g., a software token) either in parallel or only if the fingerprint is not sufficiently similar. If used in parallel, the ME becomes a third authentication factor granting nonintrusiveness and consistency of the environment. If the second factor is used only in doubt, the ME becomes the de facto second factor. It also grants nonintrusiveness and the consistency of the environment but in addition lifts the user's burden to engage in the second authentication factor actively. The service can request a fingerprint at any time. Only the fingerprint's length, t seconds, limits the interval to conduct authentication. Our results suggest that the service can attempt authentication at least every minute (see Sect. 4.3).

5.2   Factor Strength

To determine the strength of our authentication factor, we compute the amount of information in terms of Shannon entropy H [24]. The entropy in our scheme resides in the APRs of a fingerprint. Each APR has a theoretical upper bound of 63 bits according to the specifications [8]. However, the measurable entropy of APRs will only be a fraction of these possibilities. Therefore, we calculate a minimum estimate based on the APRs of the $187, 200$ fingerprints observed in our data set. We get a minimum entropy of $H(MAC) = 10.45$ bits considering the observed MAC addresses. We take the joint entropy of dependent variables into account for the capability features before summing them together. This results in $H(Flags, WPA, RSN) + H(Frequency, Bitrate) + H(Mode) = 9.1$ bits of minimum entropy per APR expressed in terms of its capability features. To estimate a lower bound for the entropy provided in one fingerprint, we need to consider the number of observed APs. In our data set, each fingerprint contains one to forty-two APs. Therefore, each fingerprint $\mathbf{F}$ provides at least $9.1 \times |\mathbf{APR(F)}|$ bits of entropy when using the capability features.

5.3   Adversary Model and Security Analysis

Masquerading is the main threat against any authentication scheme. For fingerprinting MEs this implies to get data that the service accepts as a valid fingerprint. We look specifically at attacks of acquiring a fingerprint. We consider the compromise of the user devices as an orthogonal problem and assume that known device protection techniques are in place, such as the regular installation of security updates. Furthermore, we assume that a public-key infrastructure (PKI) is in place to guarantee that the service is eligible to query the user's ME and that the communication channel is TLS [6] protected.

Brute Force. An adversary can try to guess the fingerprint of the user. The recommendations of the NIST has varying factor-strengths based on the factors themselves; a user-chosen password requires a minimum of 48 bits, a key for an attestation of a sensor-modality in the biometric context a minimum of 112 bits [19]. Fingerprinting the ME resides somewhere between. It is not arbitrarily chosen by the user like a password, but can and will change unlike biometric features. Assuming a minimum of six APs, an adversary has to brute force at least 2^{54} possibilities, which is larger than the entropy recommendations for passwords. Even if the adversary can guess a fingerprint, the first and second authentication factors are still in place.

Compromise Template Confidentiality. An adversary can try to compromise the user's template by taking control of the service. What can be done is not to store the user's template $\mathbb{F}$ in plaintext. The only information required in plain text is the RSSI value to compare its distance to a newly obtained RSSI value. However, the RSSI value is not identifying. Storing a salted and hashed representation of each APR, congruent to the password case, is insufficient. The entropy of an individual APR is too low. Knowing the salt, the adversary could brute force the hash. An alternative is the salted-challenge-response authentication mechanism (SCRAM). The crucial point is that SCRAM applies a password-based key derivation function (PBKDF2), which uses a client-side salt to increase the entropy. Using SCRAM solves the low entropy problem of a single APR. To not further burden the user by requiring him to store a salt for each observed APR, we assume the user will use his first AF password as salt input to each PBKDF2. Note that this does not violate key separation as the reused password is used as salt to the PBKDF2, while each observed APR is used as the 'password'. The guarantees provided by SCRAM can then be transferred to a set of APRs.

Compromise the Communication Channel. An adversary can also try to attack the communication channel. In a successful attack, the confidentiality of the exchanged information would be compromised. In the registration phase, this exchanged information contains the user's template; during the login phase, it contains a fingerprint. First, the assumption of a TLS-protected communication channel comes into mind. However, even if the TLS is broken or circumvented, applying SCRAM stops an adversary from attacking the communication channel. SCRAM exchanges several hashed messages between the user and the service that are not susceptible to replay attacks. It authenticates the client to the server and the server to the client.

On the Intrinsic Threat of Local Adversaries. Using location as an authentication factor has the intrinsic property that everyone at the location classifies as being at the location. Therefore, we assume that our authentication factor is only used in conjunction with existing authentication factors. The authors of [3] claim to define a location with an accuracy of 2 m based on the RSSI difference $d(\mathbb{F})$ when combining WiFi with Bluetooth data. We intend to investigate the boundaries of an ME by WiFi with a suitable dataset in the future. However, being on location is limited to a very restricted set of adversaries who also need to acquire the other authentication factors.

Too Few APs in the ME. If a template contains too few (less than six) APs, the service should advise against using the ME as an authentication factor because the entropy is too low. Our experiments show that our classification works for locations with only a single AP. However, the security guarantees are insufficient. Our results show with a precision of 1 that we do not grant authentication in a situation in which authentication should have been denied.

6 Comparison with Related Work

Continuous authentication systems in the literature are based on the physical activities [1] or biometric features of the user [17]. Behavioral biometrics also include the routines of a user. Several works consider building such routine profiles of a user's day from WiFi. The authors of [20] restrict their profile creation to the SSID of only the AP to which the user is connected. They also use several other sensor readings. The authors of [14] apply a similar approach to large available datasets. The authors of [18] compare application usage, Bluetooth, and WiFi signals. They report stable rates above 90% for WiFi over one week using the combination of MAC, SSID, and RSSI, showing that our expectation of the consistency of WiFi APs is valid. In Table 1, we compare our results with the related literature (reporting the accuracy). This comparison shows two significant differences compared to our approach. First, all works from the literature use more sensors than just WiFi sensors. Second, all works using WiFi sensors use the identifying features (MAC address or SSID), which are unique, but privacy sensitive. If at least six APs are available, our mechanism outperforms the results reported in the literature with an accuracy of 0.996. We achieve this while only taking capability features and no PII into account. All other works build upon potentially privacy-invasive data. One explanation might be that we do not focus on creating a user's behavioral profile. Doing so is just one application of using the ME as an authentication factor. Also, setting a minimum of observed APs explains our slight edge in performance. The closest result reported [20] takes only a single connected AP into account, and the second closest [3] focuses only on the top-ranked network nodes (determined by the RSSI value).

Table 1. Comparison of our mechanism with results from the literature in location fingerprinting in terms of the signals used, the type of features used, and the reported accuracy.

Study	Signal	Feature	Accuracy
Ours ($\#AP \geq 6$)	WiFi	Capability	0.996
[20]	WiFi, BT, GPS, usage	Identifying	0.994
[3]	WiFi, BT	Identifying	0.984
Ours	WiFi	Capability	0.984
[14]	WiFi, App, various	Identifying	0.983
[18]	WiFi, BT, App	Identifying	0.85

Several works in the literature propose to use APs and their beacon frames to authenticate a user's location. Despite pretty good results, all of these works require a change of the beacon frame itself. Cho et al. [5] propose a protocol to allow location-aware access control by defining a location area enclosed by overlapping ranges of multiple APs. They derive a location key from the overlapping APs' beacon frame information but require the APs to include a nonce into their beacon frames and communicate them via a secured channel among themselves. Bao [4] proposes a solution assuming an additional key server next to the user and APs. Saroiu et al. [23] go even one step further and suggest adding two functionalities to the AP. Their AP must be capable of generating a location certificate and engaging in an exchange protocol on the user's behalf. Pham et al. [21] observed this issue and suggested reducing its surface by relying on a centrally coordinated distributed AP infrastructure by proposing to rely on existing WiFi APs operated as hotspots owned by the WiFi network providing company. Our solution differs from these, as we do not require the AP to send content in the beacon frame that exceeds the beacon frame standard [9].

7   Discussion and Future Work

Changes in the ME. Signal availability is a problem for all radio communications. However, the results of [18] suggest consistency of at least one week for WiFi signals, and we expect that APs are far less frequently changed. We believe that an AP is more likely to be exchanged by the user switching ISPs than reconfiguration, which occurs less than annually per AP. Even if some APs change, our classifier construction allows for tolerance in the composition of signals. If the ME changes too much, the user should update the template by re-enrolling an ME. The first and second authentication factors provide the authenticity of the user in this scenario.

Keeping the APRs Confidential. A fruitful future work might be to introduce a user-specific secret S and not store the APRs in plain text but a cipher text after encryption under S. Using a user-specific secret S has the downside that this secret must be securely stored on the user's device. However, it would serve at least three purposes: Firstly, MAC addresses and other PII may be used because they are unretrievable from a cipher text without knowing the secret S but will most likely improve the classifier's performance. Secondly, the problem of local adversaries being capable of plainly conducting a measurement of the user's location becomes impossible as such an adversary would be required to get hold of S. Thirdly, a chain of trust links a measured environment to a user. The cipher text would be constructed from the measurement of the ME and the user-specific secret S. This binds the measurement to the secret S. Assuming that S is stored securely on the device, the cipher text is bound to the device. If the device is bound to the user either by knowledge or biometry, there is a chain of trust, from a measurement to a cipher text, from the cipher text to a device, and from the device to the user.

Behavioral user Profiles. Another direction to look into is the user's behavior. When a user consistently uses a service by authenticating via the ME, it could become possible to build a behavioral profile (e.g., between 09.00 and 10.00 AM, the user recurringly logs in from the same ME during workdays). Creating a behavioral profile is a double-edged sword. On the one hand, it could improve the precision of an authentication claim, and the system could learn those behavioral patterns to increase the likelihood of authenticating the correct user. On the other hand, there might be contexts where the service should not learn about a user's template correlation. A future direction to look into is building these profiles or preventing the service from knowing which template a user's claim matches.

Further Directions. We envision further research in evaluating the perimeters of MEs to understand how close a fingerprint must be to an ME to match a template and, thus, how close an adversary must be to gather a matching fingerprint. Moreover, we see interesting future work in using the entropy in an ME's fingerprint to harden an existing authentication factor.

8 Conclusion

We introduce a nonintrusive authentication factor based on the user's measurable environment (ME). We aim for simplicity and consistency while respecting the privacy of the user. Simplicity is provided by lifting the burden for the user to perform extra tasks for multi-factor authentication (e.g., retype SMS tokens on every login). We respect the user's privacy by conducting this authentication in our instantiation only based on capability features and by only recognizing a known ME instead of mapping the user to a geographical location.

We show that a WiFi fingerprint (not containing PII) can be classified with a precision of 1 and a recall above 0.99 when observing multiple APs. A precision of 1, no false positives, enables us to apply the concept of WiFi fingerprinting to authentication since no wrongful authentication gets conducted. A recall above 0.99 implies that our mechanism correctly authenticates a valid user most of the time, which is tolerable as we assume a first and second factor as a backup for authentication. We rely on APs that are ubiquitously present in any WiFi environment. We require only a few kilobytes of data to be transmitted, and the classification requires only a low amount of complexity. We perform the classification of an ME by computing the JSR of a newly obtained fingerprint to a known template and using it as a nonintrusive authentication factor.

References

1. Abuhamad, M., Abuhmed, T., Mohaisen, D., Nyang, D.: AUToSen: deep-learning-based implicit continuous authentication using smartphone sensors. IEEE Internet Things J. **7**(6), 5008–5020 (2020)
2. Al-Naji, F.H., Zagrouba, R.: A survey on continuous authentication methods in internet of things environment. Comput. Commun. **163**, 109–133 (2020)
3. Alawami, M.A., Kim, H.: LocAuth: a fine-grained indoor location-based authentication system using wireless networks characteristics. Comput. Secur. **89**, 101683 (2020)
4. Bao, L.: Location authentication methods for wireless network access control. In: 2008 IEEE International Performance, Computing and Communications Conference, pp. 160–167 (2008)

5. Cho, Y., Bao, L., Goodrich, M.T.: LAAC: a location-aware access control protocol. In: 2006 3rd Annual International Conference on Mobile and Ubiquitous Systems-Workshops, pp. 1–7 (2006)
6. Dierks, T.: TLS v 1.2 (2008). http://www.hjp.at/doc/rfc/rfc5246.html
7. Gassend, B., Clarke, D., Van Dijk, M., Devadas, S.: Silicon physical random functions. In: Proceedings of the 9th ACM Conference on Computer and Communications Security, pp. 148–160 (2002)
8. GNOME. org.freedesktop.networkmanager.accesspoint (2021). https://developer.gnome.org/NetworkManager/1.2/gdbus-org.freedesktop.NetworkManager.Access Point.html
9. IEEE Standard. Wireless LAN medium access control (MAC) and physical layer (PHY) specifications (2007). https://www.iith.ac.in/tbr/teaching/docs/802.11-2007.pdf
10. Intel. Dual band wireless-ac 8265 (2021). https://ark.intel.com/content/www/us/en/ark/products/94150/intel-dual-band-wireless-ac-8265.html
11. ISO 27000. Information technology, security techniques, information security management systems, overview andvocabulary (2018)
12. Jaccard, P.: Étude comparative de la distribution florale dans une portion des alpes et des jura. Bull. Soc. Vaudoise Sci. Nat. **37**, 547–579 (1901)
13. Jeong, W., et al.: SDR receiver using commodity WiFi via physical-layer signal reconstruction. In: Proceedings of the 26th Annual International Conference on Mobile Computing and Networking, pp. 1–14 (2020)
14. Kayacik, H.G., Just, M., Baillie, L., Aspinall, D., Micallef, N.: Data Driven Authentication: On the effectiveness of user behaviour modelling with mobile device sensors (2014)
15. Lebovic, N.: Biometrics, or the power of the radical center. Crit. Inq. **41**(4), 841–868 (2015)
16. McKenna, S.J., Gong, S.: Non-intrusive person authentication for access control by visual tracking and face recognition. In: International Conference on Audio-and Video-Based Biometric Person Authentication, pp. 177–183 (1997)
17. Mosenia, A., Sur-Kolay, S., Raghunathan, A., Jha, N.K.: CABA: continuous authentication based on BioAura. IEEE Trans. Comput. **66**(5), 759–772 (2017)
18. Neal, T.J., Woodard, D.L., Striegel, A.D.: Mobile device application, bluetooth, and Wi-Fi usage data as behavioral biometric traits. In: 2015 IEEE 7th International Conference on Biometrics Theory, Applications and Systems (BTAS), pp. 1–6 (2015)
19. NIST. Digital identity guidelines, authentication and lifecycle management (2021). https://pages.nist.gov/800-63-3/sp800-63b.html
20. Pang, X., Yang, L., Liu, M., Ma, J.: Mineauth: mining behavioural habits for continuous authentication on a smartphone. In: Australasian Conference on Information Security and Privacy, pp. 533–551 (2019)
21. Pham, A., Huguenin, K., Bilogrevic, I., Dacosta, I., Hubaux, J.-P.: SecureRun: cheat-proof and private summaries for location-based activities. IEEE Trans. Mob. Comput. **15**, 08 (2016)
22. Rudd, E.M., Boult, T.E.: Caliper: continuous authentication layered with integrated PKI encoding recognition. In: Proceedings of the IEEE Conference on Computer Vision and Pattern Recognition Workshops, pp. 127–135 (2016)
23. Saroiu, S., Wolman, A.: Enabling new mobile applications with location proofs. In: Proceedings of the 10th Workshop on Mobile Computing Systems and Applications, pp. 1–6 (2009)

24. Shannon, C.E.: Prediction and entropy of printed English. Bell Syst. Tech. J. **30**, 50–64 (1951)
25. Vinh, N.X., Epps, J., Bailey, J.: Information theoretic measures for clusterings comparison: variants, properties, normalization and correction for chance. J. Mach. Learn. Res. **11**, 2837–2854 (2010)
26. Wen, M., Hanwen, L.: Radar detection for 802.11 a systems in 5 GHz band. In: Proceedings of 2005 International Conference on Wireless Communications, Networking and Mobile Computing, vol. 1, pp. 512–514. IEEE (2005)
27. WP29. Opinion 01/2017 on the proposed regulation for the eprivacy regulation (2002/58/EC) (2017)

Protecting FIDO Extensions Against Man-in-the-Middle Attacks

Andre Büttner[✉] and Nils Gruschka

University of Oslo, Gaustadalléen 23B, 0373 Oslo, Norway
{andrbut,nilsgrus}@ifi.uio.no

Abstract. FIDO authentication has many advantages over password-based authentication, since it relies on proof of possession of a security key. It eliminates the need to remember long passwords and, in particular, is resistant to phishing attacks. Beyond that, the FIDO protocols consider protocol extensions for more advanced use cases such as online transactions. FIDO extensions, however, are not well protected from Man-in-the-Middle (MitM) attacks. This is because the specifications require a secure transport between client and server, but there exists no end-to-end protection between server and authenticator.

In this paper, we discuss MitM scenarios in which FIDO extensions may be intercepted. We further propose an application-layer security protocol based on the CBOR Object Signing and Encryption (COSE) standard to mitigate these threats. This protocol was verified in a formal security evaluation using ProVerif and, finally, implemented in a proof-of-concept.

Keywords: Security · FIDO · WebAuthn · CTAP2 · COSE · Encryption

1 Introduction

In today's digital era, almost everybody is used to log in to a website with a password. Although passwords are easy to use, they have many disadvantages in terms of security. They are often easy to guess or sometimes publicly disclosed after a data breach. Furthermore, passwords are vulnerable to phishing attacks. Therefore, many services already implement multi-factor authentication.

FIDO authentication is a relatively young technology that intends to overcome the disadvantages of passwords. The basic idea behind it is to use an authenticator device as a more secure authentication factor, either in addition to or even as a replacement for passwords. A feature that is rarely used yet but may become important soon are FIDO extensions. These allow for more advanced functionality beyond simple authentication. FIDO authentication may, for example, be used to confirm online purchases or banking transactions. Initially, a FIDO Transaction Confirmation extension was proposed, which includes a human-readable text representation of a transaction as an extension [13]. This extension, however, was never implemented and already became deprecated. It

A. Saracino and P. Mori (Eds.): ETAA 2022, LNCS 13782, pp. 70–87, 2023.
https://doi.org/10.1007/978-3-031-25467-3_5

is replaced by the more recent Secure Payment Confirmation [27]. We expect to see more different kinds of extensions like this in the future.

However, the FIDO specifications do not provide any specific protection for FIDO extensions. Since extensions can contain very sensitive information, it should be ensured that attackers cannot intercept or manipulate this information. There are several possibilities for attackers to act as Man-in-the-Middle (MitM). The FIDO protocols only protect the integrity of messages from the authenticator to the server. The integrity of messages from the server cannot be checked by the authenticator. While this is not necessary for basic authentication, this may be crucial for certain extensions. Also, confidentiality cannot be guaranteed as there is no encryption on the application layer.

To mitigate the risk of manipulation or disclosure of FIDO extensions, we propose to apply authenticated encryption to FIDO extensions. In this paper, we provide the following contributions:

1. An overview of different MitM attack scenarios against FIDO extensions.
2. A proposal for a security protocol to protect FIDO extensions.
3. A formal security verification of this protocol.
4. A proof-of-concept implementation.

The remainder of this paper is structured as follows. Section 2 gives an overview of FIDO authentication and the COSE protocol. In Sect. 3 related literature on FIDO is presented. The attack model addressed in this paper is explained in Sect. 4. In Sect. 5 we specify our proposed security protocol, which is evaluated in Sect. 6. In Sect. 7 we describe a proof-of-concept implementation. A discussion of the proposed solution is provided in Sect. 8. Our findings are summarized in Sect. 9 along with a brief outlook on future work.

2   Background

In this section we firstly provide some background information on FIDO authentication. Afterwards the CBOR based COSE protocol is described.

2.1   FIDO Authentication

The Fast IDentity Online (FIDO) Alliance is publicly active since 2013 [16]. Today it includes members from several popular Internet companies. Their main objective is to provide industry standards for using authenticators to authenticate against web applications either as a single factor (password-less) or as an additional factor (2FA/MFA). There are two different types of authenticators. *Roaming authenticators* are external security tokens (for example a YubiKey) that can be connected via USB, Bluetooth-Low-Energy (BLE) or Near-Field-Communication (NFC). In contrast to this, *platform authenticators* are integrated into client devices like computers and smartphones.

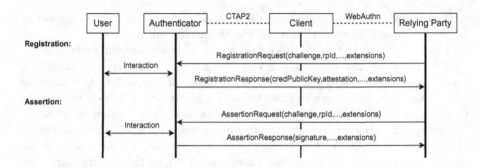

Fig. 1. FIDO authentication overview.

In this paper, we mainly focus on FIDO2, which consists of the Web Authentication (WebAuthn) API and the Client-to-Authenticator-Protocol 2 (CTAP2) [15]. WebAuthn has become a W3C standard [22] and defines a JavaScript API and data structures that can be used to create credentials and get assertions from the authenticator. CTAP2 defines the protocol between the client platform and the authenticator.

For FIDO authentication, security and trust are based on public key cryptography. Figure 1 gives a brief overview of the different roles and messages that are specified for FIDO2 authentication. At first, an authenticator (e.g. a security token) needs to be registered at a web service, the so-called relying party (RP). When a user registers at a RP, the RP firstly sends a registration request to the authenticator which includes a random nonce (challenge), its identifier (rpId), and further parameters. The authenticator creates a credential key pair and shares its public key with the RP by sending a registration response. In addition, the authenticator may include an attestation certificate that verifies the origin of the authenticator by a certified manufacturer. For this purpose, the FIDO Alliance provides a public service called *Metadata Service* [14], which contains a list of vendors, their public keys and their certification levels. During authentication, the RP creates another challenge value and sends it to the authenticator in an assertion request. This challenge is signed by the authenticator, along with other parameters, using the private key of the credential that was previously registered with the RP. Using the corresponding public key, the RP can verify the signature of the assertion response. Both for registration and authentication, the user needs to interact with the authenticator, e.g., by pressing a button. For more security, the user can enter a PIN or interact with a biometric scanner, which provides an additional authentication factor.

The FIDO specifications leave room for additional features by using protocol extensions. Extensions sent by the RP to the authenticator are called *input extensions* and extensions from the authenticator to the RP *output extensions*. Furthermore, it is distinguished between *client extensions* and *authenticator extensions*. In this paper, we focus on authenticator extensions, i.e., those that are processed by the authenticator. Several different types of extensions have been proposed (see e.g. [20]), however, almost none of these has been implemented yet. The Secure Payment Confirmation [27] is a new W3C specification and describes a payment extension for FIDO authentication. It is a good example of more advanced applications of FIDO authentication. However, it must be kept in mind that such an extension also requires high security standards.

2.2 COSE

The *CBOR Object Signing and Encryption* (COSE) [33] protocol aims to provide a standard for exchanging signed and encrypted data in the *Concise Binary Object Representation* (CBOR) [6] format. CBOR is a binary data format that is particularly useful for low-resource devices due to its lightweight and efficient design. Among other things, it is used in the CTAP2 protocol. Data can be structured into maps and arrays of various types. Consequently, JSON objects can be easily converted to CBOR objects, which makes it also usable from a developer's perspective. Furthermore CBOR provides features like tags and flexible map and array lengths.

COSE is basically adapted from the JavaScript Object Signing and Encryption (JOSE) protocol. It defines data structures for exchanging data that is signed, encrypted or authenticated (MAC). COSE objects carry the payload together with additional information about the keys and algorithms that are used. A COSE message is composed of a CBOR array that contains a protected header, an unprotected header, the payload and depending on the type additional values like the signature or the message authentication tag. A protected header is a CBOR encoded map of certain header values. It is used as input in addition to the actual payload for cryptographic functions, e.g., as additional authenticated data (AAD) when using authenticated encryption or as input for the signature. The unprotected header is a map that contains further header values, which in contrast to the protected header are not cryptographically bound to the payload or signature. COSE signature messages may contain one (`COSE_Sign1`) or multiple signatures (`COSE_Sign`). Encryption messages can be intended for one recipient (`COSE_Encrypt0`) or for multiple recipients (`COSE_Encrypt`). Respectively, there are also two different COSE MAC structures.

The COSE protocol does not specify, how keys are negotiated by the different parties. However, it defines a *COSE Key* structure which contains all necessary information for a key. This can be useful, e.g., for storing the key or for sending it to another party in a standardized manner. For example, the FIDO2 protocols make use of the COSE Key format to send the public key from the authenticator to the RP. There currently exists a draft for a COSE based *Ephemeral Diffie-Hellman Over COSE* (EDHOC) protocol to provide additional features like key negotiation [34], which, however, is not standardized yet.

3 Related Work

Since FIDO authentication is a fairly new topic, research on the subject is still very limited. We therefore provide a brief overview of the related literature.

There has been quite some research on the usability of FIDO authentication [28,29]. One of the major concerns by the users is the account recovery. If the authenticator gets lost, there must be some way to regain access to the account. At the same time, the recovery option should not reduce the security. As a solution, an enhancement for the protocol was proposed that enables the use of a backup key that only needs to be configured once in the beginning [17]. Furthermore, a study on different account recovery approaches was conducted to compare them in terms of usability, deployability and security [23]. Other researchers applied formal methods to analyse the security of the FIDO protocols [3,11]. In particular, there still seems to be a lack of research that focuses on the CTAP2 protocol.

There has also been done little research specifically on the security of FIDO extensions. For example, it was proposed to use structured data formats for FIDO Transaction Confirmation to facilitate the validation of transaction information by the authenticator thereby making it more secure [8]. Furthermore, some researchers have pointed out that the FIDO Transaction Confirmation extension is vulnerable to manipulation. They propose to let an RP sign the transaction information, which can be validated on the client-side in a trusted environment [37,38]. However, they do not point out how the authenticity of the public key is guaranteed. In addition to this, we see further risks. If FIDO extensions can be manipulated, they can also be eavesdropped in similar attack scenarios. Therefore, confidentiality should be equally considered alongside integrity and authenticity.

4   Attacker Model

The WebAuthn standard [22] requires a so-called secure context, which includes the use of HTTP over TLS (HTTPS). This ensures that the client can verify the authenticity of a web server. Yet, there are more components involved that can interfere with FIDO messages beyond client and server. We therefore argue that HTTPS does not provide sufficient protection for FIDO messages at all. FIDO authentication can involve several different intermediaries between the RP and the authenticator. These include (1) web proxies between the client and the RP, (2) the client application, (3) intermediary processes on the client platform and (4) hardware between a roaming authenticator and the client device. Thus, there is a significantly large attack surface, as illustrated in Fig. 2.

Plain authentication—also referred to as *entity authentication*—without any extensions is not likely at risk, because the protocol is designed not to contain sensitive information. Also, it is resistant against manipulation through the challenge-response protocol. However, authentication that involves extensions exchanged between the RP and the authenticator may contain valuable information, e.g., personal data, transaction details or other sensitive information. Such information could be obtained or manipulated by an adversary. In the following, we elaborate on the four different MitM scenarios in more detail.

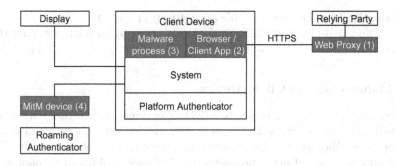

Fig. 2. Attack surface: possible points of interception are highlighted.

4.1 Vulnerable Web Intermediaries

Distributed systems like web applications typically include intermediaries such as content delivery networks (CDN), load balancers or web application firewalls (WAF). The secure context requirement mentioned above can only be verified for the connection between a browser and the next HTTP entity. As a consequence, it cannot be guaranteed that intermediaries communicate with other intermediaries or the server via HTTPS. Apart from that, HTTPS is only protecting on the transport layer. Web intermediaries usually operate on the application layer and therefore need to access HTTP messages including the body. Consequently, they are able to read FIDO messages in clear text.

If a proxy behaves maliciously, this can have severe security implications. A proxy could be misused to intentionally read FIDO messages and disclose sensitive information. Beyond that, a malicious proxy could manipulate extensions. There is no integrity check considered for FIDO messages from the RP to the authenticator. Depending on the type or use of an extension, only a user may notice the manipulation through manual inspection. For messages from the authenticator to the RP, any manipulation will be detected by the RP, since the authenticator data including extensions are signed. In any case, there is still the risk of information disclosure.

Another concern with HTTP intermediaries is the possibility of attacks that result from the semantic gap of the HTTP protocol [9]. In particular, cache poisoning vulnerabilities could be exploited to disclose FIDO messages. This can be realized by various techniques like request smuggling [26] or web cache deception [18].

4.2 Compromised Client Application

The client application on the user's device may be running in a browser as a JavaScript application or a native mobile application. Both browser clients and native mobile applications often use third-party libraries. If not checked properly, such libraries can include malicious code [2,39]. Another possibility to compromise the client application is to exploit cross site scripting (XSS) vulnerabilities in a JavaScript application to inject code that intercepts FIDO messages and modifies extensions or forwards them to an untrustworthy third party.

4.3 Malware on the Client Device

Malware can pose a further threat to FIDO extensions. An attacker may be able to install malicious software on a user's client device through an email attachment or some other exploit. By intercepting inter-process communication (IPC) or accessing memory of other processes, the malware could read or manipulate FIDO messages. Moreover, it could bypass security measures by the browser and system and send its own FIDO assertions to the authenticator. It was already shown that this can cause a user to confirm a malicious transaction [7]. In addition, there may be specific types of viruses targeting browsers on client devices. By this, a browser may be corrupted in a way that it can be controlled by an attacker, which is also known as Man-in-the-Browser (MitB) attacks [10]. Beyond that, platform authenticators are generally at risk of behaving unintentionally when they are affected by malware. This can be mitigated with the use of trusted platform modules (TPM), which make sure that secret keys are not disclosed. Nevertheless, exploits against extensions remain a threat.

4.4 MitM Between Client Device and Authenticator

With respect to roaming authenticators, an attacker may try to intercept the connection between the client device and the authenticator. This is certainly a more difficult attack, since an attacker needs physical access to the user's devices. One could argue that the security of the FIDO device is completely compromised in that case and other MitM countermeasures would be pointless. However, this is only true for authenticators that just require a button press and not when the authenticator uses a more secure verification method such as biometrics.

Even if an authenticator uses a verification method like biometrics, an attacker may still be able to intercept the connection and eavesdrop or manipulate extensions. For example, there are known MitM attacks against Bluetooth [24,35]. NFC is very unlikely to be intercepted without the owner's awareness. But still, a potential attack against NFC has been demonstrated [1].

5 Protocol Design

As shown in the previous section, FIDO messages can indeed be vulnerable to several attacks. Extensions may include sensitive information and are at risk of being modified by or disclosed to unauthorized parties. Considering the large attack surface, we see the necessity to apply further measures. In this section, we present our proposed protocol to protect FIDO extensions.

5.1 Authenticated Encryption

Sensitive FIDO extensions should provide secure properties such as confidentiality, integrity and authenticity. Messages sent from the authenticator to the RP are already signed and, thus, do not require any additional authentication. However, messages from the RP to the authenticator are neither signed, nor authenticated by any means. Xu *et al.* [37] suggest that the relying party shall sign extensions. In their approach the verification of the signature is done on the client device and the public key for verifying the signature is given by the TLS connection. We, however, want to enable the authenticator itself to validate the authenticity of extensions from the RP.

Since signatures do only provide integrity and authenticity, but no confidentiality, we propose to fulfill all these properties by using authenticated encryption (AE) instead. For this the RP and the authenticator must firstly agree upon a shared secret during registration. After that they can derive key material from the shared secret and use AE algorithms such as AES-GCM to encrypt and authenticate extensions that are included in assertion messages.

There can be multiple authenticators registered with one user account on the RP. However, there will be a different shared key between the RP and every authenticator. The RP does not know which registered authenticator will be used for the assertion. Therefore we need to apply *key wrapping*. This means that the actual extension is encrypted with a newly created content encryption key. This key is then encrypted with the shared key and appended to the message for each authenticator. For encrypting the extensions in the assertion response by the authenticator the shared key can be used directly, because the message is only intended for the RP. This is formalized in our model in Sect. 6.2.

5.2 Key Exchange

Encrypting FIDO extensions requires the RP and the authenticator to exchange keys in advance. Normally, a public-key infrastructure (PKI) is used to create certificates which provide trust and authenticity for exchanged keys. Hardware tokens, however, are very limited and likely not powerful enough in terms of storage and computation to handle certificate chains. Since they operate offline, there is also no possibility for them to directly interact with certificate authorities over the network (e.g. to check on certificate revocations). This is different for other types of authenticators with more computing resources and networking capabilities. However, we want to address all types of authenticators with our solution. Because of this, we consider the *trust-on-first-use* authentication scheme [36]. This means that we trust the first connection between authenticator and RP not being intercepted by an adversary.

To generate a shared secret, the RP and the authenticator perform a Diffie-Hellman key exchange (DHKE) during the registration. The RP includes the first part of the DHKE as registration input extension. The authenticator generates and stores the shared secret from the DHKE and sends a registration response to the RP, which includes the second part of the DHKE as registration output extension. Finally, the RP generates the shared secret from the DHKE and stores it together with the newly registered credential.

The (unauthenticated) DHKE is known to be secure against eavesdropping, but vulnerable to active MitM attacks. Authenticators use attestations that should be validated by RPs to create a certain amount of trust. If properly done, this can mitigate active MitM attacks. However, for higher security, it is important that the authenticator includes both parts of the DHKE in its attestation signature, as shown in Sect. 6.1.

5.3 Data Format

A further important aspect is the format used to exchange the encrypted data along with required metadata like an input vector (IV) and the algorithm used. FIDO authenticator extensions must be provided in the CBOR format. As described in Sect. 2.2, the accompanying protocol for signature and encryption is COSE. Since the public key from the authenticator is transmitted as a COSE key, authenticators and RPs are both supporting parts of the COSE protocol already. The COSE standard supports encryption for single and multiple recipients, and thus provides all functionality needed for the proposed protocol. Our suggestion is therefore to embed extensions in COSE structures. The COSE key format can also be used to encode the DH public keys that are exchanged during the registration to generate the shared secret.

5.4 Displaying User Information

When encrypting extensions, we still need to be able to display information, such as transaction information, to the user in a secure manner. This is the key aspect of the What-You-See-Is-What-You-Sign principle [25]. The different possible architectures with FIDO authenticators are displayed in Fig. 3. Ideally, an authenticator should provide a secure display (Fig. 3a). However, there are no roaming authenticators with a display on the market yet. In most cases, the client platform would be responsible for displaying the information to the user. With our approach, the client will not be able to decrypt the extensions on transit. Therefore, the authenticator firstly needs to decrypt the extensions and then forward the user information to the client display on a secure path (Fig. 3b). For this the platform should provide appropriate measures to ensure that there is no interception possible when displaying the information to the user.

Platform authenticators are integrated into computers or smartphones. Since these already have a display, platform authenticators can provide the decrypted user information instantly to the platform without an intermediary connection (Fig. 3c). FIDO authentication is already supported by most platforms like Windows [21], MacOS/iOS [30] and Android [19]. The platform itself must ensure that the information that is displayed to the user has not been modified by another malicious process. When the client device is responsible for displaying the information, there are further risks like UI deception attacks [4,12], which,

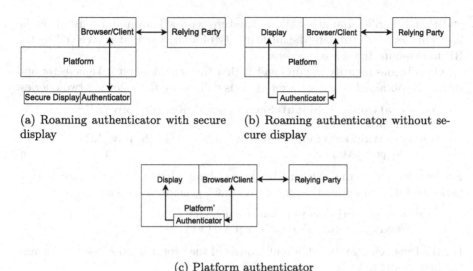

(a) Roaming authenticator with secure display

(b) Roaming authenticator without secure display

(c) Platform authenticator

Fig. 3. Architectures for different types of authenticators.

however, must be taken care of by the operating system. The same applies when a roaming authenticator without a secure display is used.

6   Security Evaluation

ProVerif [5] is a common protocol verifier that uses Horn-clause based representations of a protocol and the applied π-calculus for process verification. A formal model of the protocol and the security properties to be tested are defined in input files. The output are the test results indicating whether the defined security properties are met. If a test fails, a possible attack trace is provided. This tool has been used to conduct a security evaluation of our protocol.

Formal models have been created for the key exchange during the registration of an authenticator and for the exchange of encrypted and authenticated extensions. A basic description of the models, some code excerpts and the results are given below. For more details, the sources and results of the evaluation can be found in our Github repository[1].

6.1   Key Exchange

In our protocol, a DHKE is performed to generate a shared secret on the relying party and the authenticator. Even though a client can verify the TLS certificate of a RP, we assume that an authenticator cannot validate the authenticity of a RP. However, we consider that a RP requires attestation from the authenticator

---

[1] https://github.com/Digital-Security-Lab/protecting-fido-extensions-proverif.

and that it verifies the attestation signature with a known and trusted public key. This serves to validate the authenticity of a DH key that is received by the RP to compute the shared secret.

One obvious security requirement is that the shared secret is kept secret and cannot be obtained by an attacker. This is defined by the following two queries:

```
query attacker (computeSecret (publicKey (dh_priv_AU) ,
    dh_priv_RP)) .
query attacker (computeSecret (publicKey (dh_priv_RP) ,
    dh_priv_AU)) .
```

Further, we check the authenticity by verifying that a key exchange is only performed if both authenticator and RP have generated the same secret:

```
query x:G;  inj−event (sharedSecretRP (x))
    ==>inj−event (sharedSecretAU (x)) .
```

For the key exchange, two different models of the protocol were created, because the first model did not pass the verification.

Protocol Model 1. In this model, the authenticator creates an attestation signature including the nonce, the credential public key and the output extension containing its DH key:

```
sign (( nonce , credPubKey ,dh_pub_AU) , privKeyAttestation)
```

This signature is verified by the RP against the original nonce, the credential public key and the extension with the DH key by the authenticator:

```
checksign (( nonce , credPubKey ,dh_pub_AU) , signature ,
    pubKeyAttestation)
```

When verifying this model with ProVerif, the authenticity test fails. The detailed output of ProVerif contains a trace where an attacker intercepts a registration request by the RP and replaces the DH key of the RP with its own key. Because of this, the authenticator will compute a different shared secret than the RP. As a consequence, the authenticator cannot authenticate or decrypt assertion extensions from the RP, but from the attacker. However, the attacker cannot gain much from this, except for causing a denial of service. Nonetheless, this attack should be avoided.

Protocol Model 2. In the second model, the authenticator includes both DH keys in the attestation signature, so the RP can verify that the same shared secret is computed on both ends. From a theoretical perspective, it would be enough to only modify the signature. However, in practice the protocol proposed here should be compatible with the FIDO standards. Therefore the authenticator will have to include both its own DH key and the DH key from the RP in the output extensions, so both keys are implicitly included in the signature:

```
sign (( nonce , credPubKey ,dh_pub_AU,dh_pub_RP) ,
    privKeyAttestation)
```

The same is true when verifying the signature. In particular, the RP must check the signature with its own generated DH key and the authenticator's key:

checksign ((nonce , credPubKey , dh_pub_AU , dh_pub_RP) , signature , pubKeyAttestation)

With this model all tests succeed and the secrecy of the shared secret is guaranteed as well as the authenticity of the public keys that were exchanged. We therefore consider this model in our final solution.

6.2   Encrypted Assertion Extensions

The second critical part of the proposed protocol is the exchange of encrypted and authenticated extensions between RP and authenticator during assertions. We make the following assumptions. First, the authenticator is successfully registered with the RP. This means that the RP has the credential public key of the authenticator to verify its signature and both authenticator and RP have exchanged a shared secret and derived from it a shared key. Second, while replay attacks against the RP are prevented by the nonce, replay attacks against the authenticator are not.

A security requirement here is the secrecy of input and output extensions, which is defined in the following two queries:

query attacker (AssertionInputExtensions) .
query attacker (AssertionOutputExtensions) .

In addition, the authenticator and the RP should both only accept authenticated extensions. An attacker must not be able to forge or manipulate extensions in a way that they are processed by either of them. As mentioned above, we assume an attacker to be able to replay assertion messages to the authenticator, but not to the RP. Therefore only events in connection with output extensions are defined as injective events:

query x : bitstring ; **event** (receiveInputExtensionsAU (x))
  ⟹**event** (sendInputExtensionsRP (x)) .
query x : bitstring ; **inj−event** (receiveOutputExtensionsRP (x))
  ⟹**inj−event** (sendOutputExtensionsAU (x)) .

This time only one model had to be created. In this model, the RP uses key wrapping to transmit a content encryption key together with the encrypted input extensions:

new cek : key ;
let inputExtensions_enc = **senc** (AssertionInputExtensions , cek) **in**
let cek_enc = **senc** (key2Bitstring (cek) , sharedKey) **in**
out (c , (nonceRP , cek_enc , inputExtensions_enc))

The authenticator, on the other hand, uses the shared key directly to encrypt the output extensions:

```
let outputExtensions_enc = senc(AssertionOutputExtensions,
    sharedKey) in
```

The evaluation of this model with ProVerif indicates that the expected security requirements are met and no attacks have been found. Hence, with this model, we can successfully exchange FIDO extensions while preserving their confidentiality, integrity, and authenticity.

7 Implementation

A proof-of-concept (PoC) application has been developed to demonstrate how to implement essential parts of the proposed protocol. The sources and further instructions can be found in a Github repository[2]. Since FIDO keys can be, e.g., USB devices with very limited resources, it was decided to provide a test application using the C programming language and libraries that are optimized for embedded devices. To implement the protocol, a CBOR library is needed, which is already included in each FIDO component, as it is required for implementing the basic FIDO protocols. Moreover, a COSE library is needed. Since we could not find a useful implementation, we developed an open-source COSE library[3] based on the RFC 8152 standard [33]. At the time of writing, this library is still a work in progress, but already provides everything needed for the proposed protocol. Finally, additional crypto libraries may be needed to do certain operations such as generating private and public keys, to compute the shared secret from the DHKE and to derive key material using e.g. a Hash Key Derivation Function (HKDF).

The PoC application is meant to demonstrate the parts that have to be implemented in addition to the FIDO protocols. Basic features such as credential creation, attestation and signature verification are therefore not included. For the DHKE, elliptic curve key pairs were used. The authenticated encryption is done using AES-GCM with a 128-bit key. In the example application, it is firstly shown how the RP and the authenticator exchange a shared secret. The RP creates the first part of the DHKE, which is encoded in a COSE Key structure and transmitted to the authenticator. The authenticator then creates the second part of the DHKE, computes the shared secret and derives from it a 128-bit key using a HKDF with SHA-256 as underlying hash function. Subsequently, the RP receives the second part of the DHKE (in a real world application together with the first part of the DHKE as discussed in Sect. 6.1) and analogously computes the shared secret and derives from it a key the same way as the authenticator. In the second part of the application, the RP is provided with the credential identifier and the shared key of an authenticator. The RP creates an encoded COSE Encrypt structure that contains an extension value encrypted with a content encryption key. This key is then encrypted using the shared key and attached as a recipient object. The credential id of the corresponding authenticator is used as

---

[2] https://github.com/Digital-Security-Lab/protecting-fido-extensions-poc.
[3] https://github.com/abuettner/cose-lib.

key identifier. The authenticator receives this COSE Encrypt structure and identifies that a recipient is attached with its credential id. It can then decrypt the content encryption key and finally the extension value. The authenticator then creates an encoded COSE Encrypt0 structure that contains another extension value, this time encrypted with the shared key. The RP receives this structure and finally decrypts the extension value by the authenticator. Note that in a real application, the RP can identify the shared key used by the credential id that is part of the authenticator data.

Preliminary measurements on a Raspberry Pi Pico (264 kB SRAM, 2 MB on-board flash memory) [31] show that the steps performed by an authenticator during the registration take about 250 ms, while the steps during the assertion take about 5 ms. The additional delay during registration is acceptable, since this is performed only once per application. The additional runtime on assertions would be unnoticeable by the user.

8 Discussion

In this section we discuss our proposed protocol for protecting FIDO extensions with regard to several different aspects.

8.1 Security

There are several different ways to intercept FIDO messages in clear text as described in Sect. 4. This allows an attacker to intercept FIDO extensions with valuable information and either eavesdrop or manipulate them. As shown by the evaluation the security of FIDO extensions can be significantly improved with our proposed solution. However, the security of extensions also depends on a secure key exchange. While RPs can verify the attestation to get information on security properties provided by an authenticator to create trust, authenticators cannot reliably verify the origin of a RP. In our formal models, the client between the RP and the authenticator has not been considered. It could be argued that the client adds security to some extent, e.g., by validating the TLS certificate of the server. Yet, this is not sufficient and additional measures as proposed in this paper are justified.

The security also depends on the strength of cryptographic algorithms. This has not been evaluated within this work. We consider cryptographic algorithms that are widely accepted and used e.g. in the most recent TLS 1.3 [32]. However, the proposed protocol is meant to be generic, so cryptographic algorithms can simply be replaced if necessary (e.g. with post-quantum cryptography).

8.2 Implementation

We provide an example on how our protocol can be implemented. Our protocol is completely compatible with the FIDO standards. While the protocol is quite complex, our implementation can be used to integrate it into FIDO applications with low effort. Since there are not too many COSE library implementations, a further contribution of this work is such a COSE library which can be used by any other C application.

At the time of writing, FIDO implementations are quite restricted to standardized extensions. Even though the WebAuthn standard [22] defines how arbitrary extensions should be forwarded to the authenticator, browsers have not implemented this. This means that custom extensions are not passed to FIDO devices. It is therefore challenging to implement a real-world example at this stage. Our protocol should also be considered for extensions that will be standardized in the future, such as, the Secure Payment Confirmation [27] which is clearly an extension with high security requirements.

8.3   Usability

Usability is an important aspect that can affect the user experience and acceptance. It is an essential criterion that will certainly determine how successful FIDO authentication will become in the future. The usability for FIDO authentication is, however, not affected by our proposed protocol. The protocol requires a key exchange and subsequent encryption of FIDO extensions, which happens autonomously and is therefore unnoticed by the user.

9   Conclusion and Outlook

The FIDO protocols are a promising way to prevent security risks that arise with password authentication. However, we describe several MitM attacks which show that FIDO extensions are vulnerable to disclosure and manipulation. In order to mitigate such attacks, we propose a protocol that secures FIDO extensions by authenticated encryption. While our methodology includes some challenges such as the initial key exchange and displaying user information for authenticators without a secure display, we see a considerable security gain and aim for a standardized way to secure any kind of FIDO extension.

There are not many extensions used in practice yet. Nevertheless, the standardization process of the Secure Payment Confirmation indicates that we can expect more extensions to appear in the near future. At the time of writing, it is still under discussion if arbitrary extensions should be allowed or not. We argue that it would be beneficial from a developer's perspective to be able to add extensions for different applications. This should, however, be done with security in mind. The protocol presented in this paper could provide a way to satisfy this requirement. In future work, we will test our approach in real world scenarios. Furthermore, we are working on a lab environment that will facilitate practical research with FIDO authentication.

References

1. Akter, S., Chellappan, S., Chakraborty, T., Khan, T.A., Rahman, A., Al Islam, A.A.: Man-in-the-middle attack on contactless payment over NFC communications: design implementation, experiments and detection. IEEE Trans. Depend. Secur. Comput. **18**, 3012–3023 (2020)
2. Arshad, S., Kharraz, A., Robertson, W.: Include me out: in-browser detection of malicious third-party content inclusions. In: Grossklags, J., Preneel, B. (eds.) FC 2016. LNCS, vol. 9603, pp. 441–459. Springer, Heidelberg (2017). https://doi.org/10.1007/978-3-662-54970-4_26
3. Barbosa, M., Boldyreva, A., Chen, S., Warinschi, B.: Provable security analysis of FIDO2. In: Malkin, T., Peikert, C. (eds.) CRYPTO 2021. LNCS, vol. 12827, pp. 125–156. Springer, Cham (2021). https://doi.org/10.1007/978-3-030-84252-9_5
4. Bianchi, A., Corbetta, J., Invernizzi, L., Fratantonio, Y., Kruegel, C., Vigna, G.: What the app is that? Deception and countermeasures in the android user interface. In: 2015 IEEE Symposium on Security and Privacy, pp. 931–948. IEEE (2015)
5. Blanchet, B.: Modeling and verifying security protocols with the applied pi calculus and ProVerif. Found. Trends® Priv. Secur. **1**(1–2), 1–135 (2016)
6. Bormann, C., Hoffman, P.E.: Concise Binary Object Representation (CBOR). RFC 8949, December 2020. https://doi.org/10.17487/RFC8949, https://rfc-editor.org/rfc/rfc8949.txt
7. Bui, T., Rao, S.P., Antikainen, M., Bojan, V.M., Aura, T.: Man-in-the-machine: exploiting ill-secured communication inside the computer. In: 27th USENIX Security Symposium (USENIX Security 2018), pp. 1511–1525 (2018)
8. Büttner, A., Gruschka, N.: Enhancing FIDO Transaction Confirmation with Structured Data Formats. In: Norsk IKT-konferanse for forskning og utdanning. No. 3 (2021)
9. Büttner, A., Nguyen, H.V., Gruschka, N., Lo Iacono, L.: Less is often more: header whitelisting as semantic gap mitigation in HTTP-based software systems. In: Jøsang, A., Futcher, L., Hagen, J. (eds.) SEC 2021. IAICT, vol. 625, pp. 332–347. Springer, Cham (2021). https://doi.org/10.1007/978-3-030-78120-0_22
10. Dougan, T., Curran, K.: Man in the browser attacks. Int. J. Amb. Comput. Intell. (IJACI) **4**(1), 29–39 (2012)
11. Feng, H., Li, H., Pan, X., Zhao, Z.: A formal analysis of the FIDO UAF protocol. In: Proceedings of 28th Network And Distributed System Security Symposium (NDSS) (2021)
12. Fernandes, E., et al.: Android UI deception revisited: attacks and defenses. In: Grossklags, J., Preneel, B. (eds.) FC 2016. LNCS, vol. 9603, pp. 41–59. Springer, Heidelberg (2017). https://doi.org/10.1007/978-3-662-54970-4_3
13. FIDO Alliance: FIDO Transaction Confirmation White Paper. Technical report, August 2020. https://media.fidoalliance.org/wp-content/uploads/2020/08/FIDO-Alliance-Transaction-Confirmation-White-Paper-08-18-DM.pdf
14. FIDO Alliance: Fido alliance metadata service (2021). https://fidoalliance.org/metadata/
15. FIDO Alliance: Fido alliance specifications overview (2021). https://fidoalliance.org/specifications/
16. FIDO Alliance: History of fido alliance (2021). https://fidoalliance.org/overview/history/

17. Frymann, N., Gardham, D., Kiefer, F., Lundberg, E., Manulis, M., Nilsson, D.: Asynchronous remote key generation: an analysis of Yubico's proposal for W3C WebAuthn. In: Proceedings of the 2020 ACM SIGSAC Conference on Computer and Communications Security, pp. 939–954 (2020)
18. Gil, O.: Web cache deception attack. Black Hat USA 2017 (2017)
19. Google: Fido2 API for android (2020). https://developers.google.com/identity/fido/android/native-apps
20. Group, W.W.A.W.: Web authentication (webauthn) (2020). https://www.iana.org/assignments/webauthn/webauthn.xhtml
21. Jakkal, V.: The passwordless future is here for your microsoft account (2021). https://www.microsoft.com/security/blog/2021/09/15/the-passwordless-future-is-here-for-your-microsoft-account/
22. Kumar, A., Jones, J., Hodges, J., Jones, M., Lundberg, E.: Web authentication: an API for accessing public key credentials - level 2. In: W3C recommendation, W3C, April 2021. https://www.w3.org/TR/2021/REC-webauthn-2-20210408/
23. Kunke, J., Wiefling, S., Ullmann, M., Lo Iacono, L.: Evaluation of account recovery strategies with fido2-based passwordless authentication. In: Roßnagel, H., Schunck, C.H., Mödersheim, S. (eds.) Open Identity Summit 2021, pp. 59–70. Gesellschaft für Informatik e.V, Bonn (2021)
24. Lahmadi, A., Duque, A., Heraief, N., Francq, J.: MitM attack detection in BLE networks using reconstruction and classification machine learning techniques. In: Koprinska, I., et al. (eds.) ECML PKDD 2020. CCIS, vol. 1323, pp. 149–164. Springer, Cham (2020). https://doi.org/10.1007/978-3-030-65965-3_10
25. Landrock, P., Pedersen, T.: WYSIWYS?-What you see is what you sign? Inf. Secur. Techn. Rep. 3(2), 55–61 (1998)
26. Linhart, C., Klein, A., Heled, R., Steve, O.: HTTP Request Smuggling (2005). https://www.cgisecurity.com/lib/HTTP-Request-Smuggling.pdf
27. McGruer, S., Solomakhin, R.: Secure Payment Confirmation. In: W3C working draft, W3C, August 2021. https://www.w3.org/TR/2021/WD-secure-payment-confirmation-20210831/
28. Owens, K., Anise, O., Krauss, A., Ur, B.: user perceptions of the usability and security of smartphones as FIDO2 roaming authenticators. In: Seventeenth Symposium on Usable Privacy and Security (SOUPS 2021), pp. 57–76 (2021)
29. Pfeffer, K., et al.: On the usability of authenticity checks for hardware security tokens. In: 30th USENIX Security Symposium (USENIX Security 2021) (2021)
30. Porter, J.: Safari to support password-less logins via face id and touch id later this year (2020). https://www.theverge.com/2020/6/24/21301509/apple-safari-14-browser-face-touch-id-logins-webauthn-fido2
31. Raspberry Pi Ltd: Raspberry Pi Documentation - Raspberry Pi Pico (2022). https://www.raspberrypi.com/documentation/microcontrollers/raspberry-pi-pico.html
32. Rescorla, E.: The Transport Layer Security (TLS) Protocol Version 1.3. RFC 8446, August 2018. https://doi.org/10.17487/RFC8446, https://rfc-editor.org/rfc/rfc8446.txt
33. Schaad, J.: CBOR Object Signing and Encryption (COSE). RFC 8152, July 2017. https://doi.org/10.17487/RFC8152, https://rfc-editor.org/rfc/rfc8152.txt
34. Selander, G., Mattsson, J.P., Palombini, F.: Ephemeral Diffie-Hellman Over COSE (EDHOC). Internet-Draft draft-ietf-lake-edhoc-12, Internet Engineering Task Force, October 2021. https://datatracker.ietf.org/doc/html/draft-ietf-lake-edhoc-12. (work in Progress)

35. Sun, D.Z., Mu, Y., Susilo, W.: Man-in-the-middle attacks on secure simple pairing in Bluetooth standard V5. 0 and its countermeasure. Pers. Ubiquit. Comput. **22**(1), 55–67 (2018)
36. Wendlandt, D., Andersen, D.G., Perrig, A.: Perspectives: improving ssh-style host authentication with multi-path probing. In: USENIX Annual Technical Conference, vol. 8, pp. 321–334 (2008)
37. Xu, P., Sun, R., Wang, W., Chen, T., Zheng, Y., Jin, H.: SDD: a trusted display of FIDO2 transaction confirmation without trusted execution environment. Future Gener. Comput. Syst. **125**, 32–40 (2021)
38. Zhang, Y., Wang, X., Zhao, Z., Li, H.: Secure display for FIDO transaction confirmation. In: Proceedings of the Eighth ACM Conference on Data and Application Security and Privacy, pp. 155–157 (2018)
39. Zhang, Z., Diao, W., Hu, C., Guo, S., Zuo, C., Li, L.: An empirical study of potentially malicious third-party libraries in Android apps. In: Proceedings of the 13th ACM Conference on Security and Privacy in Wireless and Mobile Networks, pp. 144–154 (2020)

Authentication, Authorization, and Selective Disclosure for IoT Data Sharing Using Verifiable Credentials and Zero-Knowledge Proofs

Nikos Fotiou[1]([✉]), Iakovos Pittaras[1], Spiros Chadoulos[1,2], Vasilios A. Siris[1], George C. Polyzos[1], Nikolaos Ipiotis[2], and Stratos Keranidis[3]

[1] Mobile Multimedia Laboratory, Department of Informatics School of Information Sciences and Technology Athens University of Economics and Business, Evelpidon 47A, 113 62 Athens, Greece
{fotiou,pittaras,spiroscha,vsiris,polyzos}@aueb.gr
[2] Plegma Labs, Neratziotissis 115, 15124, Marousi Athens, Greece
{sc,ni}@pleg.ma
[3] DomX IoT Technologies, Stratigou Sarafi 48E, 55133 Thessaloniki, Greece
stratos@domx.io

Abstract. As IoT becomes omnipresent vast amounts of data are generated, which can be used for building innovative applications. However, interoperability issues and security concerns, prevent harvesting the full potentials of these data. In this paper we consider the use case of data generated by smart buildings. Buildings are becoming ever "smarter" by integrating IoT devices that improve comfort through sensing and automation. However, these devices and their data are usually siloed in specific applications or manufacturers, even though they can be valuable for various interested stakeholders who provide different types of "over the top" services, e.g., energy management. Most data sharing techniques follow an "all or nothing" approach, creating significant security and privacy threats, when even partially revealed, privacy-preserving, data subsets can fuel innovative applications. With these in mind we develop a platform that enables controlled, privacy-preserving sharing of data items. Our system innovates in two directions: Firstly, it provides a framework for allowing discovery and selective disclosure of IoT data without violating their integrity. Secondly, it provides a user-friendly, intuitive mechanisms allowing efficient, fine-grained access control over the shared data. Our solution leverages recent advances in the areas of Self-Sovereign Identities, Verifiable Credentials, and Zero-Knowledge Proofs, and it integrates them in a platform that combines the industry-standard authorization framework OAuth 2.0 and the Web of Things specifications.

1 Introduction

IoT systems generate vast amounts of data nevertheless, their potential is limited by security and privacy concerns, as well as by the lack of interoperability.

© Springer Nature Switzerland AG 2023
A. Saracino and P. Mori (Eds.): ETAA 2022, LNCS 13782, pp. 88–101, 2023.
https://doi.org/10.1007/978-3-031-25467-3_6

A striking example is the case of smart buildings. Smart buildings employ a variety of IoT devices that generate data which support various applications, such as energy management, automations, security and safety, etc. These applications are in most cases siloed and the generated data are only used for the specific purposes of each application. Nevertheless, these data can be valuable for a variety of stakeholders that are able to deliver value-added services for other domains. Energy suppliers represent a key stakeholder that can significantly benefit from both energy and non-energy data that can be collected, either directly by smart building systems or even by legacy systems that are integrated with smart IoT equipment. According to an Accenture study [11], energy utilities will need to master data analytics in the near future, to continue developing valuable, customer-focused products that go far beyond old business models and plain commodity offerings. Data analytics can benefit energy utilities in multiple ways: a) successful retention of customers through the delivery of innovative personalized services, b) improved customer targeting and segmentation through consumer profiling, c) improved energy market participation through demand forecasting based on machine learning, d) improved energy savings for end users through optimized demand management and many others.

On the other hand, end-users would be interested in securely making a subset of the data generated by their IoT devices available to these 3rd parties, in a stratified manner, to benefit from the added value of the provided services. Nevertheless, several challenges have to be overcome: a) a uniform and standardized way for advertising/discovering, requesting, and transmitting data should be in place, b) sensitive information should be stripped from the shared data without violating data integrity and provenance, c) an efficient, usable mechanism for expressing and enforcing fine grained access control policies should be available, d) data access rights should be expressed in a rich and verifiable manner. In addition to overcoming these challenges, proposed solutions should encourage interoperability and prevent vendor "lock-in". With these in mind we designed, implemented, and evaluated *SelectShare*: a platform for controlled sharing of IoT data, focusing on smart buildings.

SelectShare is a system that makes available data from IoT systems located in buildings, and facilitates fine-grained, privacy-preserving data access to controlled subsets of these data, while at the same time ensuring data integrity, provenance verification, authenticity, and interoperability with different types of systems. This is achieved by integrating four components. First, an IoT gateway that exposes a data access API by following W3C's Web of Things specifications [13] facilitating data discovery and data interoperability. Second, a data transcoder that collects data from IoT devices, transcodes them into JSON objects, and signs them using a digital signature scheme that enables selective disclosure of the claims included in the JSON, providing at the same time Zero-Knowledge Proofs (ZKPs) of their integrity. Third an OAuth 2.0 [9] based Verifiable Credential (VC) [15] issuing mechanism for generating self-contained, fine-grained access tokens. Finally, an HTTP-proxy that acts as a Policy Enforcement Point (PEP), for controlling access to the IoT gateway, as well as for selectively hiding parts of the responses generated by the gateway. Using this approach, SelectShare achieves fine-grained access control with minimal overhead and no modification to the IoT devices.

The remainder of this paper is structured as follows. In Sect. 2, we introduce our enabling mechanisms and we discuss related work in this area. In Sect. 3, we detail the design of our architecture. In Sect. 4, we present the implementation and evaluation of our solution. We conclude our paper in Sect. 5.

2 Background and Related Work

2.1 Verifiable Credentials

A *Verifiable Credential* (VC) [15] allows an *issuer* to assert some *attributes* about an entity referred to as the VC *subject*. A VC includes information about the issuer, the subject, the asserted attributes, as well as possible constraints (e.g., expiration date). Then, a VC *holder* (which is usually the same entity as the VC subject) can prove to a *verifier* that it owns a VC with certain characteristics. This is usually achieved by including in the VC an identifier (e.g., a public key), owned by the holder that enables the holder to generate a *proof of possession* (e.g., a digital signature with the corresponding private key). The VC verification process does not require communication with the VC issuer.

The VC data model allows different VC *types*, which define the attributes a VC should include. This provides great flexibility, since VC integrators can define their own types that fit the purposes of their systems. Our system uses a new VC type named *CapabilitiesCredential* that "describes" which portion of a data item a user can access.

2.2 BBS+ Digital Signatures

BBS+ is a digital signature protocol which is used for signing an *array* of messages. It was first envisioned by [2] (from where it takes its name), touched again in [1], re-visited in [3] and is currently under standardization [25]. BBS+ provide the ability to sign an array of individual messages, with only a single *constant size* signature. The signature can be validated given the signer's *Public Key* (PK) and the entire array of signed messages; this is equivalent to validating a "traditional" digital signature, if we consider the array of messages as a single compound message.

BBS+ can be combined with Zero-Knowledge Proofs (ZKP) allowing an entity to selectively hide elements of singed array of messages. In particular, *any* entity that knows the signature and the original signed array of messages, can create a proof of knowledge of the signature while selectively disclosing only a sub-array of the signed messages. The proof size will be linear to the number of un-revealed messages. The proof can be validated with only the signer's public key and the array of revealed messages.

2.3   Related Work

Related systems are using "attribute-based access control" (ABAC) (e.g., [5,8]) for achieving similar goals. With ABAC, users own a "token" that includes their attributes. Then, a "policy decision point" (PDP) decides whether a user can perform a requested operation based on a list of pre-configured access control policies. Our system follows an alternative approach: our proposed solution is in essence a "capabilities-based access control" system where users own a token that describes their capabilities. The main advantage of this approach is that it removes the need for access control lists. On the other hand, we recognize that ABAC is useful when access control decision involves user context; in this case the policy decision process should receive as input attributes related to the context of the user. Our proxy can be easily extended to include related mechanisms (e.g., the system presented in [18]). Similarly our proxy can be extended to accommodate aspects such as user behavior (e.g., the solution presented in [7]).

Many systems leverage the blockchain technology to achieve similar targets (e.g., [19,20]). We postulate that blockchain overhead cannot be tolerated by a system like ours and a trusted proxy that would mediate the communication between the blockchain and our system would be required: this trusted proxy would negate any decentralization advantages of the blockchain technology. It should be highlighted that many VC systems rely on a blockchain to achieve their security properties. However, VCs in our solution do not need any blockchain-based system.

Kratos (initially described in [21] and then extended in [22]) is a system that wants to achieve similar goals as our solution for home IoT environments, where an IoT device may be owned by multiple users who may define different access control policies. Our solution considers that each IoT device is owned by a single entity, hence our approach is simpler. Additionally, Kratos proposes its own, specific mechanisms for expressing policies and rights, whereas our system relies on existing, open standards; hence our solution can be easily integrated in existing deployments.

Our solution assumes that IoT devices produce correct data and it does not consider any countermeasure against malicious IoT device owners. Our solution can be complemented by existing solutions that incentivize IoT device owner to provide correct data (e.g., [16]). Finally, in our solution, the used HTTP proxy is trusted to disclose the appropriate information; other related works rely on cryptographic constructions for not requiring this trust relationship (e.g., the work in [23] relies on "Attribute-based encryption"). However, this comes with the cost of additional computational overhead, as well as with the overhead of managing encryption keys.

Our solution extends our previous work presented in [6]. In SelectShare, we consider gateways that interconnect IoT devices that may be owned by different entities. Additionally, SelectShare assumes that the data generated by the IoT devices has been collected, singed, and stored in a storage node, prior being requested. Finally, SelectShare leverages ZKPs in order to provide even finer-grained access control.

3   Architecture

SelectShare architecture (also illustrated in Fig. 1) considers collections of IoT devices the belong to the corresponding IoT device *owner* (e.g., IoT devices of a smart building). These devices produce *measurements* that the device owners wish to share with 3rd party data *clients* (e.g., analytics services). Data sharing is implemented through a single gateway, administrated by an independent service *provider* that can be accessed by clients using a standardized API. This gateway retrieves data from a *storage node*, which acts as a data repository, populated by specialized data *transcoders*. The communication between a client and the gateway is intercepted by a proxy which is responsible for validating client access rights, as well as for hiding parts of the response generated by the gateway. Clients' access rights are expressed using a Verifiable Credential (VC) issued by a VC issuer.

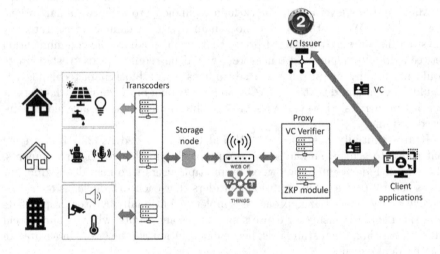

Fig. 1. Overview of the SelectShare architecture

SelectShare considers a setup phase during which: device owners configure VC issuers with the corresponding access control policies, and the proxy is configured with a list of trusted issuers per IoT device owner.

3.1   Data Encoding and Signing

In order to facilitate data sharing, SelectShare architecture considers an entity, named *transcoder*, which transcodes the data produced by each IoT device based on a predefined JSON *schema*. In our particular instantiation a generated JSON file includes: i) an IoT device specific identifier and ii) a list of measurements, where each measurement includes a device-unique measurement identifier (called *field*) and a list of *value-time* pairs. The following listing is an example of a generated JSON file.

```
1  {
2     "deviceID":"monitor−1",
3     "measurements":[
4        {
5        "field":"temperature",
6        "values":[
7            "time":"1658162155",
8            "value":"30C"
9            ]
10       },
11       {
12       "field":"humidity",
13       "values":[
14           "time":"1658162155",
15           "value":"50"
16           ]
17       },
18    ]
19 }
```

Listing 1.1. A JSON file produced by a transcoder

It should be highlighted that depending on the requirements of a SelectShare deployment, different schemas can be considered. A transcoder is owned and managed by the corresponding IoT devices owner, i.e., a transcoder interacts with the IoT devices of a specific owner. Additionally, each transcoder is configured with a BBS+ signing key and each generated JSON file is singed using BBS+ (by the transcoder). Finally, singed JSON files are stored in a storage node, administrated by the service provider.

Specific fields of a JSON file can be accessed over HTTP, through Select-Share's gateway, which implements Web of Things (WoT) Things Description (TD) [17] specifications. The WoT architecture attempts to structure well-known web protocols and tools for connecting IoT devices to the Web. In the WoT architecture communication model, IoT devices (real ones or virtual) are made available through REST-based APIs. To improve the interoperability and usability of IoT platforms, the WoT model uses a common format for describing IoT devices referred to as the Thing Description (TD). TD is a JSON-LD encoded file that includes metadata information about the IoT device (such as its id, a title, security definitions, etc.), and defines API endpoints that can be used for accessing/invoking a device's properties, actions, and events.

3.2 Authentication and Authorization Request

The VC issuer is an OAuth 2.0 authorization server extended with VC issuing capabilities. Issued VCs are encoded as JSON Web Tokens (JWT) and signed using JSON Web Signatures (JWS) (based on Sect. 6.3 of [15]), improving compatibility and integration with existing tools. SelectShare considers VCs that describe which "measurements" of the IoT devices of a particular owner, a client can access. These VCs are generated based on policies defined by the corresponding IoT device owner. Additionally, a SelectShare VC issuer maintains a VC revocation list by implementing [14]. In particular, an issuer maintains a revocation list that concerns all non-expired VCs it has issued. This list is a simple bitstring and each VC is associated with a position in the list. Revoking a VC means setting the value of the bit corresponding to the VC equal to 1. Furthermore, each generated VC includes a field named "revocationListIndex" that specifies the position of the credential in the revocation list. Finally, a VC issuer is configured with client *credentials* (a client identifier and a client secret in our implementation), as well as with access control policies that map a client identifier to the corresponding access rights.

A client requests from the issuer a VC. A VC request is in essence an OAuth 2.0 access token request using the client credentials grant (Sect. 4.4 of [9]), (in our implementation the corresponding client identifier and secret are used as the "credentials grant"). Additionally, the client generates a public-private key pair and instructs the issuer to include the generated public key in the issued VC. This is achieved using OAuth 2.0 Rich Authorization Requests [24]. In particular, the corresponding OAuth 2.0 access token request, is extended to include the generated public key (encoded as a JSON Web Key (JWK) [10]) and a digital signature generated using the corresponding private key. The issuer authenticates the client based on the included grant and generates a VC.

A VC is the base64url encoding of a JWT singed by the issuer, according to the VC data model. The generated JWT includes a *cnf* field, as specified by RFC 7800, that contains the public key generated by the client and included in the corresponding request. The VCs used in SelectShare are of type "CapabilitiesCredential". This type includes an array, called "capabilities", and each element of this array is a map that maps an IoT device identifier to a list of measurements the client can access. An example of a VC before encoding follows (the signature part is omitted).

```
1      {
2          "jti": "https://issuer.com/credentials/1",
3          "iss": "https://issuer.com",
4          "aud": "owner−1"
5          "iat": 1617559370,
6          "exp": 1618423370,
7          "cnf": {
8            "jwk": <client jwk>
9            },
10         "vc": {
11           "@context": [
12             "https://www.w3.org/2018/credentials/v1",
13             "https://mm.aueb.gr/contexts/capabilities/v1",
14           ],
15           "type": ["VerifiableCredential"],
```

```
16              "credentialSubject": {
17                  "type": ["CapabilitiesCredential"],
18                  "capabilities": {
19                      "monitor−1": [
20                          "temperature",
21                      ]
22                  }
23              }
24          }
25      }
```

Listing 1.2. An example of a VC in our system

As it can be observed, a VC includes an identifier (the *jti* field), an identifier for the issuer (the *iss* field), an identifier for the IoT device owner (the *aud* field), an issuance and expiration time, the client public key, and the client's "capabilities". In the VC included in this example, a client can access the "temperature" measurement of "monitor-1" IoT device, owned by "owner-1".

3.3   Data Access Request

A client application requests to access some measurements of an IoT device by sending an appropriate HTTP request. This request includes the device identifier as a query parameter and a list of requested "fields" in a HTTP POST body. The HTTP request includes two HTTP headers: one that contains the JWT-encoded VC, and another that contains a *proof-of-possession* of the public key included in the VC; the latter proof is generated using OAuth 2.0 Demonstrating Proof-of-Possession at the Application Layer (DPoP) [4]. A DPoP proof is essence a JSON Web Signature (JWS) that can be verified using the public key included in the corresponding VC. The payload of the JWS is constructed using a random nonce, the HTTP request method, the HTTP request URI, and a timestamp indicating the proof's creation time.

A data access request is intercepted by SelectShare's HTTP proxy. SelectShare's HTTP proxy includes a *VC verifier*: the VC verifier examines if the request includes an appropriate VC and then it verifies the validity, the status, and the ownership of a VC. A VC is appropriate if the "aud" claim includes the identifier of the device owner and if contains the "fields" of the "deviceID" included in the request.

The validity of a VC is verified by evaluating whether: a) the VC has not expired, b) the signature of the VC is valid, c) the VC has been issued by an issuer trusted by the device owner.

The status of the VC is verified by communicating with the VC issuer, and using the validation process described in [14]. I.e., in a nutshell, the verifier retrieves the revocation list (which is a bitstring), locates the bit that corresponds to evaluated VC, and examines the value of that bit.

Finally, the ownership of a VC is validated using the DPoP proof, i.e., the verifier verifies that the proof is adequately fresh, it includes a nonce not seen before, it includes the correct HTTP method and URI, and its signature can be verified using the public key included in the VC.

3.4 Data Access Response

Upon receiving an authorized request, the proxy forwards to the gateway. The gateway retrieves from a storage node a JSON file that includes *among other things* the requested fields, and forwards to the proxy. Finally, the proxy applies the *selective disclosure* process, in order to hide the fields not included in the client request. The selective disclosure process involves two algorithms: *framing* and *canonicalization*.

Framing. Framing refers to the derivation of a "sub-item" from an item, that contains only part of the original one. Data framing is used to enable selective disclosure of the data item's information. More specifically, the framing algorithm accepts the original item and a frame as input and returns a new item that only contains the key-value pairs specified by the frame. The frame itself is a JSON structure that specifies the parts of the original item that should appear in the resulting one (and be disclosed in the end). For this purpose, the frame contains the keys that lead to the values that the prover will want to reveal. The framing algorithm used in SelectShare also includes special symbols that can be used for selecting specific elements in an array. For example, considering Listing 1.1 the following frame will reveal "the value of all measurements that include the field *temperature*":

```
1   {
2       "measurements": {
3           "*":{
4               "field":"temperature",
5               "values":{
6                   "*":{
7                       "value":""
8                   }
9               }
10          }
11      }
12  }
```

Listing 1.3. An example of frame used in SelectShare

Applying this frame in Listing 1.1 will result in the following object:

```
1   {
2       "measurements":[
3           {
4               "field":"temperature",
5               "values":[
```

```
6                    "value":"30C"
7              ]
8         }
9    ]
10  }
```

Listing 1.4. Output of framing operation

Canonicalization. As discussed previously, BBS+ signatures act on arrays of messages and not on structured data formats like JSON. In order for a transcoder to be able to sign a data item, as well as in order for the proxy to be able to derive ZKPs, data items must be canonicalized. Various canonicalization algorithms have been proposed by related efforts. A canonicalization algorithm serializes a JSON-encoded item into an array of messages, which can then be signed by a multi-message digital signature system like BBS+. There are various security requirements that those algorithms must be conformant with, in order to not compromise the security of the system. In this work, we are using the JCan algorithm [12] which is a lightweight, provably secure, JSON canonicalization proposal, designed to work with any data model.

Selective Disclosure. Any entity can generate a sub-item of a content item based on a frame and provide a ZKP that proves its correctness as follows. Initially, that entity applies the framing algorithm to derive the sub-item. After framing, the same entity canonicalizes the resulting sub-item, gets the array of messages that correspond to the revealed information (from the security properties of the canonicalization algorithm, this array is guaranteed to be a subset of the signed array that resulted from the canonicalization of the original item) and uses that array to derive a ZKP using BBS+.

The function of selective disclosure is implemented in a distributed manner by the transcoder and the ZKP module of the proxy. In particular, transcoders are responsible for signing the generated JSON objects using BBS+ signatures. The signed object is forwarded through the WoT gateway to the proxy. Then the ZKP module of the proxy is responsible for framing the signed object and for generating the corresponding ZKP. The framing operation is implemented by taking into consideration the requested "fields" option included. It should be highlighted that the proxy assumes that the user is authorized to access this field: this is true since if the user was not authorized, the incoming request would have been blocked during the VC verification process.

4   Implementation and Evaluation

We have implemented SelectShare's issuer[1] as .net core web application. Similarly we have implemented SelectShare's HTTP proxy as a Python 3 application[2].

---

[1] https://github.com/mmlab-aueb/vc-issuer.
[2] https://github.com/mmlab-aueb/py-verifier.

Finally, we implemented SelectShare's gateway based on Eclipse's Thingweb WoT gateway[3].

SelectShare introduces minimal communication overhead. VCs can be long-term (since they are bound to a public key owned by the client), hence client authorization does not have to take place often. Similarly, by using DPoP, a client can prove possession of its VC in a single message, i.e., there is no need for additional roundtrips. Moreover, the size of a VC and the corresponding proof is only few bytes. Finally, when it comes to VC status verification, a VC verifier can retrieve the revocation list once and use it for multiple requests. It is reminded that a revocation list is a bitstring that includes the status of non-expired VCs: since each VC corresponds to single bit, a revocation list may include thousands of VCs.

Similarly SelectShare introduces minimal computational overhead. VC verification process involves only the validation of two digital signatures as well as a lookup in a JSON object. Both operations are lightweight. When it comes to the overhead introduced to a proxy by the selective disclosure process we performed the following experiment in an Ubuntu 18.04 machine equipped with an intel i7-3770 CPU, 3.40 GHz and 16 GB of RAM. We constructed JSON measurement file composed of 100 fields each of which includes a single value. We calculate the time required to sign and verify sub-items that include form 1 to 99 values. Figure 2 show the signature and verification time, measured in ms. It can be observed that as the number of items included in the sub-item increases, the signature creation time decreases. This happens because for each hidden item a proxy has to perform a number of multiplications. On the other hand, the signature verification time remains almost stable. It should be noted that these measurements are obtained without any "pre-calculation", however, in a real deployment a proxy can pre-calculate many of the computations required to create a ZKP.

4.1   Security Properties

SelectShare considers the following trust relationships. An IoT device owner trusts: the VC issuer to issue an appropriate VC and correctly maintain the revocation list, the VC verifier module of the proxy to validate VCs and a proofs correctly, and the ZKP module of the proxy to not reveal "extra fields". A client trusts: the VC issuer to correctly maintain the revocation list, and the proxy to not perform "denial of service".

SelectShare facilitates security management and decreases attacks' surface. In particular, in SelectShare all access control policies are managed in a single point: the VC issuer. Adding, updating, or removing an access control policy involves no communication with the verifiers or the gateway. This is achieved by adopting the "capabilities-based access control" paradigm that removes the need for maintaining access control lists (as opposed for example to Role/Attribute-based access control). Similarly, the access control decision process is simple

---

[3] https://projects.eclipse.org/projects/iot.thingweb.

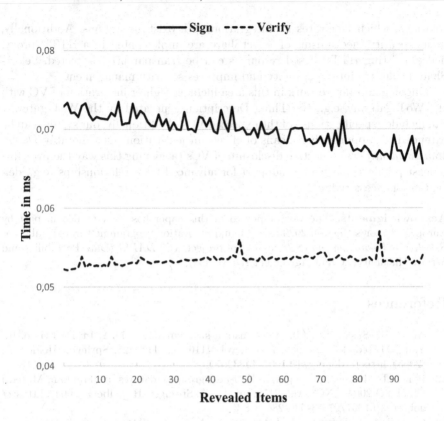

Fig. 2. Time to calculate a ZKP as a function of the revealed items

and the most "advanced" and error prone task is examining if the requested resources are included in the provided VCs. Related to that, by adopting the JWT encoding for the VCs and by relying on existing standards, our solution can leverage a plethora of existing tools that perform most of the tasks required by the access control decision process.

By adopting the ZKP-based approach for implementing selective disclosure, SelectShare provides fine-grained access control, preserving at the same time the context of the output data. For example, in a solution where each "field" in a JSON file is individually signed, additional measures must be considered in order to prevent a proxy from creating fake items by "combining" fields from different files.

5   Conclusions

In this paper we presented the design and implementation of SelectShare: an access control solution that allows fine-grained access control for IoT data sharing. SelectShare's core components are built by leveraging already standardized solutions, which facilitates its integration with existing systems. Additionally, many security mechanisms of SelectShare are implemented in a HTTP proxy, hence, existing HTTP-based resources can be transparently protected. Select-Share facilitates interoperability and improves security management.

Ongoing and future work in this area includes tighter integration of VC with the WoT gateway, e.g., the Thing Description generated by the WoT gateway can include "specifications" of the expected VCs. Additionally, our system can be extended to support other means of client authentication (most notably *Decentralized Identifiers*), selective disclosure of VCs (achieving this way the principle of least privilege), as well as support for advanced trust relationships (e.g., delegation of access rights).

Acknowledgments. The work reported in this paper has been funded in part by European Union's Horizon 2020 research and innovation programme through subgrant *Selective IoT data sharing (SelectShare)* of project *NGI DAPSI* (Data Portability and Services Incubator, Grant Agreement ID: 871498).

References

1. Au, M.H., Susilo, W., Mu, Y.: Constant-size dynamic k-TAA. In: De Prisco, R., Yung, M. (eds.) SCN 2006. LNCS, vol. 4116, pp. 111–125. Springer, Heidelberg (2006). https://doi.org/10.1007/11832072_8
2. Boneh, D., Boyen, X., Shacham, H.: Short group signatures. In: Franklin, M. (ed.) CRYPTO 2004. LNCS, vol. 3152, pp. 41–55. Springer, Heidelberg (2004). https://doi.org/10.1007/978-3-540-28628-8_3
3. Camenisch, J., Drijvers, M., Lehmann, A.: Anonymous attestation using the strong Diffie Hellman assumption revisited. In: Franz, M., Papadimitratos, P. (eds.) Trust 2016. LNCS, vol. 9824, pp. 1–20. Springer, Cham (2016). https://doi.org/10.1007/978-3-319-45572-3_1
4. Fett, D., et al.: OAuth 2.0 Demonstrating of Proof-of-Possession at the Application Layer (DPoP). RFC draft (2020). https://datatracker.ietf.org/doc/draft-ietf-oauth-dpop/
5. Dimitrakos, T., et al.: Trust aware continuous authorization for zero trust in consumer internet of things. In: 2020 IEEE 19th International Conference on Trust, Security and Privacy in Computing and Communications (TrustCom), pp. 1801–1812 (2020)
6. Fotiou, N., Siris, V.A., Polyzos, G.C., Kortesniemi, Y., Lagutin, D.: Capabilities-based access control for IoT devices using verifiable credentials. In: SafeThings 2022. IEEE (2022)
7. Ghosh, N., Chandra, S., Sachidananda, V., Elovici, Y.: Softauthz: a context-aware, behavior-based authorization framework for home IoT. IEEE Internet Things J. **6**(6), 10773–10785 (2019)
8. Goyal, G., Liu, P., Sural, S.: Securing smart home IoT systems with attribute-based access control. In: Proceedings of the 2022 ACM Workshop on Secure and Trustworthy Cyber-Physical Systems, Sat-CPS 2022, pp. 37–46. Association for Computing Machinery, New York, NY, USA (2022)
9. Hardt, D.: The OAuth 2.0 authorization framework. RFC 6749, IETF (2012)

10. Jones, M.: JSON Web Key (JWK). RFC 7517, IETF (2015). https://tools.ietf.org/html/rfc7517
11. Kaastra, M., Tinkler, S., Tuzlic, S., Abts, M., Griggiths, F., Allen, J.: New Energy Consumer. Report, Accenture (2022). https://www.accenture.com/sk-en/insights/utilities/new-energy-transition-demand
12. Kalos, V., Polyzos, G.C.: Requirements and Secure Serialization for Selective Disclosure Verifiable Credentials. In: Meng, W., Fischer-Hübner, S., Jensen, C.D. (Eds.) ICT Systems Security and Privacy Protection. SEC 2022. IFIP Advances in Information and Communication Technology, vol. 648, pp. 231–247. Springer, Cham (2022). https://doi.org/10.1007/978-3-031-06975-8_14
13. Kovatsch, M., Matsukura, R., Lagally, M., Kawaguchi, T., Toumura, K., Kajimoto, K.: Web of Things Architecture. In: W3C Recommendation, W3C (2020). https://www.w3.org/TR/wot-architecture/
14. Longley, D., Sporny, M.: Revocation list 2020. Draft Community Group Report, W3C (2021). https://w3c-ccg.github.io/vc-status-rl-2020/
15. M. Sporny et al.: Verifiable credentials data model 1.1. W3C Recommendation, W3C (2022). https://www.w3.org/TR/verifiable-claims-data-model/
16. Reijsbergen, D., Maw, A., Dinh, T.T.A., Li, W.T., Yuen, C.: Securing smart grids through an incentive mechanism for blockchain-based data sharing. In: Proceedings of the Twelfth ACM Conference on Data and Application Security and Privacy, CODASPY 2022, pp. 191–202. Association for Computing Machinery, New York, NY, USA (2022)
17. Kaebish, S., Kamiya, T., McCool, M., Charpenay, V., Kovatsch, M.: Web of Things Thing Description. W3C Recommendation, W3C (2020). https://www.w3.org/TR/wot-thing-description/
18. Schuster, R., Shmatikov, V., Tromer, E.: Situational access control in the Internet of Things. In: Proceedings of the 2018 ACM SIGSAC Conference on Computer and Communications Security, CCS 2018, pp. 1056–1073. ACM, New York, NY, USA (2018)
19. Shafagh, H., Burkhalter, L., Hithnawi, A., Duquennoy, S.: Towards blockchain-based auditable storage and sharing of IoT data. In: Proceedings of the 2017 on Cloud Computing Security Workshop, CCSW 2017, pp. 45–50. Association for Computing Machinery, New York, NY, USA (2017)
20. Shakarami, M., Benson, J., Sandhu, R.: Blockchain-based administration of access in smart home IoT. In: Proceedings of the 2022 ACM Workshop on Secure and Trustworthy Cyber-Physical Systems, Sat-CPS 2022, pp. 57–66. Association for Computing Machinery, New York, NY, USA (2022)
21. Sikder, A.K., et al.: Kratos: multi-user multi-device-aware access control system for the smart home. In: Proceedings of the 13th ACM Conference on Security and Privacy in Wireless and Mobile Networks, WiSec 2020, pp. 1–12. Association for Computing Machinery, New York, NY, USA (2020)
22. Sikder, A.K., et al.: Who's controlling my device? Multi-user multi-device-aware access control system for shared smart home environment. ACM Trans. Internet Things 3(4) (2022). https://dl.acm.org/doi/10.1145/3543513
23. Sun, Y., Yin, L., Sun, Z., Tian, Z., Du, X.: An IoT data sharing privacy preserving scheme. In: IEEE INFOCOM 2020-IEEE Conference on Computer Communications Workshops (INFOCOM WKSHPS), pp. 984–990. IEEE (2020)
24. Lodderstedt, T., et al.: OAuth 2.0 Rich Authorization Requests. RFC draft (2022). https://datatracker.ietf.org/doc/html/draft-ietf-oauth-rar
25. Whitehead, A., Lodder, M., Looker, T., Kalos, V.: The BBS signature scheme (2022). https://identity.foundation/bbs-signature/draft-bbs-signatures.html

Privacy-Preserving Speaker Verification and Speech Recognition

Wisam Abbasi[1,2]($\boxtimes$) (iD)

[1] Istituto di Informatica e Telematica, Consiglio Nazionale delle Ricerche, Pisa, Italy
`wesam.alabbasi@iit.cnr.it`
[2] Department of Computer Science at the University of Pisa, Pisa, Italy

Abstract. This paper proposes an approach to speaker verification and speech recognition in environments that require authentication and privacy protection, while accuracy and data utility must remain high. Our methodology aims at protecting audio files and users' identities through the use of encryption and hashing algorithms, while at the same time providing accurate speaker's identity prediction. In addition, for speech recognition, we introduce a mechanism to anonymize the resulting transcript of the recognized spoken language using the Named Entity Recognition method by removing sensitive entities from the text according to the user's preferences. Furthermore, a privacy-preserving version of the original audio is obtained by performing a text-to-speech translation of the anonymized transcript, which together, the anonymous audio and transcript can be transmitted to third parties or service providers without violating privacy restrictions. The proposed methodology has been validated with a set of experiments on a well-known audio dataset, the Librispeech dataset. A type of Time Delay Neural Networks, ECAPA-TDNN was used for speaker verification, Deep Speech as a type of Recurrent Neural Networks was used for speech recognition, NER for entity recognition, cryptography and hashing for privacy protection. The results demonstrate the validity of our approach to protecting the privacy of user data and biometric information while simultaneously performing data analysis with a high degree of accuracy and similarity with the results obtained with no privacy mechanisms in place, also considering the use of several privacy mechanisms.

Keywords: Authentication · Data privacy · Privacy-preserving data analysis · Speaker verification · Speech recognition

1 Introduction

Supported by the development and significant advances in Artificial Intelligence (AI) technologies, great progress has been made in the field of speech data analysis, such as the tasks of Automatic Speech Recognition (ASR), Speaker Verification, and Speaker Identification. However, these methods require relatively large

This work was partially supported by the EU H2020 project SIFIS-Home, G.A. n. 952652.

© Springer Nature Switzerland AG 2023
A. Saracino and P. Mori (Eds.): ETAA 2022, LNCS 13782, pp. 102–119, 2023.
https://doi.org/10.1007/978-3-031-25467-3_7

amounts of data for training and sample data to generate predictions. These data usually contain sensitive personal information that must remain private [22]. Privacy of individuals has become a major concern in smart environments and data analytics systems, especially with the increased processing of users' vital information. Speech data can reveal sensitive features such as the gender, age, and emotion of the speaker, as well as spoken information [39,40]. Privacy concerns vary depending on the specific task to analyze speech data, data used, infrastructure, and context. In fact, performing data analysis locally is associated with fewer privacy risks than when performing data analysis remotely, since in the second scenario the data will be transmitted to a remote server.

One of the main services provided by speech data analytics is user authentication using biometric data through the use of voice data to verify the speaker [43]. This user authentication mechanism is becoming widely used for access control, usage control, monitoring, and information retrieval applications. Voice data are used for these purposes because it is more difficult to fake, more accurate than traditional authentication mechanisms, and does not require the user to remember PINs or words. Moreover, it is more secure because it is physically connected to the user. However, biometric data analysis may be exposed to privacy leak challenges, as the user's raw biometric data can be retrieved from data stores if no protection mechanisms are in place.

Automatic speech recognition (ASR) is another example of speech data analysis and finding applications in a growing number of areas such as smart homes, e-health, journalism, voice control systems, education, business, and law [25]. Digital assistants are among the most popular speech recognition applications and are now enabled in most types of smart devices and have arrived at smart homes, the environment in which we perform our most private actions. Thus, privacy remains a major concern [7].

Privacy leakages might violate the EU proposed guidelines for the usage of artificial intelligence[1] and the GDPR regulations. Therefore, to address the privacy leakage issue, in this work, we consider a scenario in which users' audio files are either analyzed locally or transmitted to a remote server for analysis. These audio files may be leaked if any local machine, remote server, or communication medium was compromised. Therefore, we propose a framework in which privacy-preserving mechanisms are implemented both locally and on the server side so that the user can choose where to perform speech data analysis and protect sensitive information in either case. As techniques for analyzing speech data, we used both speaker verification and speech recognition models. To protect user privacy, we use encryption and hashing algorithms for identities, audio files, and generated text files. Also, we use a data anonymization technique to locate and remove sensitive information from the generated text and produce an anonymized audio file from this private text with an anonymous voice. Furthermore, we study the impact of privacy mechanisms on data utility and the accuracy of the results predicted by speech data analysis models.

---

[1] Proposal for a Regulation of the European Parliament and of the Council Laying Down Harmonised Rules on Artificial Intelligence: https://bit.ly/3y5wf6e.

The contributions of this paper are: (i) we propose a privacy-preserving speaker verification and speech recognition method as combined and standalone mechanisms relying on the protection of biometric Information Protection with encryption and data anonymization for sensitive information aimed at preserving data privacy and maintaining data utility. (ii) We define the concept of data utility using the similarity metric between original and anonymized data, then we investigate the impact of the applied privacy mechanism on the data utility. (iii) We validate our methodology through a set of experiments that include one speaker verification model and one speech recognition model with identity hashing and data encryption for biometric, text, and voice files. In addition to anonymizing text and voice data. (iv) We show and discuss how privacy mechanisms affect the accuracy and validity of the results for speaker verification and speech recognition models.

The rest of this paper is organized as follows. In Sect. 2, related work about speaker verification mechanisms, speech recognition mechanisms, and privacy-preserving data analysis is reported. Section 3 describes the reference scenario considered in this paper and the problem we are investigating. In Sect. 4 we report the proposed methodology for privacy protection with several privacy mechanisms and at different levels. Section 5 presents the experiments conducted, while Sect. 6 briefly concludes the discussion and proposes some future work directions.

2   Related Work

This section discusses some related work for speech recognition, speaker verification, and privacy-preserving techniques for both areas.

Speech Recognition and Privacy-Preserving Mechanisms. Hidden Markov Model (HMM) is one of the earliest and main models used for speech recognition through the modeling of time-varying spectral vector sequences. However, it does not consider the long-term relationships between data [19,41]. Then, Recurrent Neural Networks (RNNs) were used for speech recognition tasks with higher accuracy and better performance than the previous model, considering the dependency relationships between data items [3,14]. Convolutional Neural Networks (CNNs) were also used for speech recognition [1,42]. But, RNNs more suitable for handling temporal sequential data than CNNS, which makes them a better option for speech recognition.

Approaches proposed in the literature to protect speech data privacy fall under two categories; The first category uses cryptographic algorithms to develop speech recognition systems with privacy by design, while the second category focuses on data sanitization. On the one hand, Cryptographic methods use algorithms like CryptoNets [13], Homomorphic Encryption (HE) [24,46], Secure Multi-Party Computation (SMPC) [10,18]. On the other hand, sanitization methods anonymize speech data by modifying the emotion of the speaker's voice using

Generative Adversarial Networks (GANs) [2], random perturbation of spoken data prior to speech recognition [45], and masking the voice of the speaker [35].

Speaker Verification and Privacy-Preserving Mechanisms. Like speech recognition, several mechanisms have been used for the purposes of speaker verification, the most common of which are support Vector Machines (SVMs) [8], Probabilistic Linear Discriminant Analysis (PLDA) [20], and Gaussian Backend model [26]. But voice verification may entail concerns related to data privacy, especially when used in sensitive environments and application areas. For this reason and due to the recent legislation i.e., GDPR, several privacy mechanisms have been proposed to overcome the privacy risks associated with the speaker verification process. The main privacy methods used for privacy protection are classified as cryptographic and salting algorithms or using Federated Learning (FL) architectures [17]. Examples of cryptographic methods used with voice verification models are Homomorphic Encryption (HE) [36], Secure Multi-Party Computation (SMPC) [33], secure two-party computation (STPC) [44].

3 Reference Scenario

The reference scenario we consider in this paper is a combined approach for voice verification and speech recognition, in which data analysis can be performed locally or remotely on a *trusted server but not secure* for audio data recorded by users. The system architecture for the privacy-preserving speaker verification is presented in Fig. 1 and for the privacy-preserving speech recognition is shown in Fig. 2. Both analytics can be performed together for the same audio data or separately as stand-alone components. In both architectures, several stakeholders might record audio streams and files with microphone-enabled smart devices (Step 1). However, these stakeholders share either their personal audio data or analytics results with a remote server, and this raises privacy concerns that are solved by our proposed methodology.

For privacy-preserving speaker verification analytics in Fig. 1, on the one hand, a high computational power server is used for audio data processing and speaker verification tasks. Consequently, audio streams or files are transmitted by the smart device to the server after being encrypted to protect sensitive user information from being disclosed across the network (Step 2). On the server side, each audio file is first decrypted to get the original content and then processed to obtain speaker embedding for each person's identity that is being verified (Step 3). Then, a computation of the cosine similarity between the two embeddings is performed (Step 4), and the speaker verification model is used to predict whether the two audio files belong to the same user identity or not (Step 5). Next, the predicted results might be used to perform an action on the server side or to be encrypted and shared with the stakeholder who requested the speaker verification service (Step 6). On the other hand, if the user prefers to perform the speaker verification locally, the same data processing and analysis process used on the server side is carried out on the user side with no need to share audio data, only the encrypted identity is shared with the server if required.

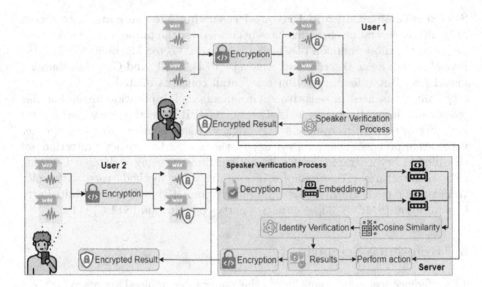

Fig. 1. Privacy-preserving speaker verification reference scenario.

For privacy-preserving speech recognition analytics in Fig. 2, a central server is also used to perform speech recognition, and audio files are transmitted with this server if the recognition task is set to be performed remotely (Step 2). Consequently, the server decrypts the received files and performs speech-to-text analysis (Step 3). Then, to protect the privacy of the user, entity recognition is used to identify sensitive entities within the recognized text (Step 4), these entities are eliminated from the text for text anonymization (Step 5). The anonymized text is then passed through the text-to-speech component to produce anonymized audio with another voice that does not reveal the identity of the original speaker (Step 6). Subsequently, the anonymized text and audio files are passed to be encrypted (Step 7). Finally, they are stored on the server and shared back with the user to be decrypted.

4   Proposed Methodology

This section discusses the methodology we defined to protect user data while performing user authentication through speaker verification in addition to speech recognition. The proposed methodology addresses the problem of protecting the privacy of user-sensitive data in applications or environments where user authentication is required and speech recognition is offered as a service. We propose a privacy-preserving approach based on *Biometric Information Protection*

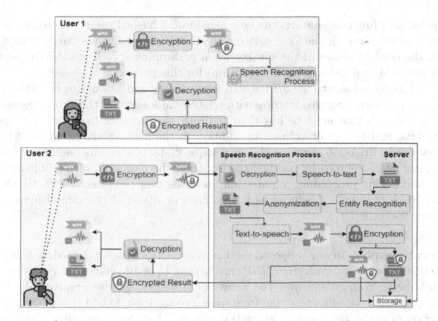

Fig. 2. Privacy-preserving speech recognition reference scenario.

with *Cryptography*. In addition to *Identity Hashing*, and *Data Anonymization* through the elimination of sensitive information for privacy protection. Moreover, we compose a speaker verification mechanism that utilizes the *ECAPA-TDNN* model and a speech recognition mechanism using the DeepSpeech model as explained in Subsects. 4.2 and 4.3.

4.1   Privacy Mechanisms Enforcement

We use four methods together to protect user data: (i) *Identity Hashing* is used to hide the named identity of the user, so that audio files or embeddings are linked to hashed names. (ii) *Cryptography* is used to protect audio and data files while they are being transferred over the network and in storage repositories. Furthermore, (iii) *Data Anonymization* is used to anonymize the textual data generated by the speech recognition model, and (iv) the original voice of the audio file is replaced by another voice for the anonymized text.

Identity Hashing. *Hashing* is a security mechanism used to produce a secured hashed output from the original input by performing some mathematical processing on the input with additional parameters so that it becomes impossible to reproduce the original input, especially since this processing is only one-way hashing. The result of the hashing function is of fixed size depending on the used hashing algorithm; for instance, using *SHA-256* generates a hash or digest with a size of 256 bits. In this work, we use identity hashing on speaker names as the hashing function converts the user name into a hashed value and stores this value on the server or the local device, and only the hashed values are compared, not the original names of the speaker when performing speech recognition, and we use *SHA-256* (Secure Hash Algorithm) for this purpose.

SHA-256 belongs to the *SHA-2* algorithms family and its working mechanism depends on some required features with relative values such as the input message or text length that must be less than 254 bits, the digest or hash length to be 256 bits, and the resulting hash in addition to the hashing algorithm must be irreversible. SHA-256 is executed in five steps, it starts with bits padding of the original data, followed by padding the length of the data, initializing buffers to be used during processing, compression, iterating over produced output till the last block of data is produced as a final hash or digest of the same length as input; 256 bits [5].

Cryptography. In our proposed methodology, *Cryptography* is used as a *Biometric Information Protection (BIP)* mechanism to secure voice files locally and while being transmitted over the network. Moreover, we use *cryptography* to secure textual data files resulting from speech recognition, in addition to the prediction made by the speaker verification model. Thus, avoiding privacy leakage and also ensuring trust by preventing data manipulation and tampering, since only users with the secret keys have access to the data. An audio file or a text file must first be encrypted before being shared or stored in a local database and decrypted after being delivered or when retrieved from the database. *Encryption* and *decryption* are performed using the keys generated by the encryption mechanism.

In this work, we used *Fernet* encryption method to be implemented in the architecture at both server and user ends with a secret, protected keys. We have selected this method because it is a light mechanism and does not require extensive computational power, so it works simply in environments with an infrastructure composed of simple devices like the IoT environments. In addition, it provides *Fernet Symmetric Encryption*, which is based on *Symmetric Encryption* provided by the most trusted encryption algorithm AES (Advanced Encryption Standard) [12,16], and is offered in a CBC (Cipher Block Chaining) mode that fulfills security requirement of encryption algorithms to ensure that every encryption of the same file or text should result with a different ciphertext by using an initialization vector [6,30]. AES is used with a 128-bit key for encryption and *PKCS7* padding. The other advantage of *Fernet* method over other methods is that it uses *SHA-256* hash algorithm [5] and *HMAC* signatures [21] for authentication so that attackers can not generate and publish bogus messages to the server. Thus, offering a more secure way for encryption and decryption that is provided by combining *AES* and *Fernet* in one method.

Data Anonymization. For data anonymization, we follow the mechanism of sensitive data recognition and elimination from input data. To produce anonymized text and anonymized audio, three steps are carried out: First, we identify sensitive data elements within the text that has been recognized by the speech recognition component using the *Named Entity Recognition* model. Then, these elements are removed from the text and replaced with the "Private Data" phrase. Furthermore, the anonymized text is converted to audio using a *Text-to-Speech* model with one unique voice other than the original speaker's voice and it can be mapped to the speaker's hashed identity. Thus, the privacy of the data and the speaker is still preserved.

Named Entity Recognition (NER) is concerned with locating key phrases and nouns in texts as entities, and these entities fall under several categories, i.e., names, locations, and addresses. The sensitivity of these entities depends on the context where the data analysis is applied. For example, names of people and locations are highly sensitive when performing data analysis and processing. However, to protect the privacy of the user, these entities can be removed from the text. Thus, still providing data valid for analysis, but without violating privacy [27].

The process for Named Entity Recognition is shown in Fig. 3. It starts with *sentence segmentation*, to split the text into sentences. Followed by *tokenization*, to split each sentence resulting from the previous step into tokens which are usually numbers, words, and punctuation marks. Next, each token is classified according to its *part-of-speech (POS)* as in Table 1. Finally, it ends with *entity detection* that classifies the word entities according to their type as an address, a time, a location, a name, etc.

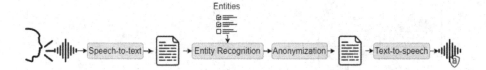

Fig. 3. Named entity recognition process.

4.2 Speaker Verification Model

For speaker verification, We use *ECAPA-TDNN* Model with the architecture shown in Fig. 4. This model was proposed in [11] and developed in *SpeechBrain* AI toolkit based on *PyTorch* [32,37]. *ECAPA-TDNN* model employs ECAPA Time Delay Neural Networks (TDNNs) derived embeddings, and it consists of an input layer, followed by a convolutional block with ReLU activation and batch normalization. Then, a sequence of three Squeeze-and-Excitation and residual blocks. Next, a convolutional block with ReLU activation. Followed by a layer that applies statistics pooling to project variable-length utterances into fixed-length speaker characterizing embeddings with batch normalization. Then a fully

Table 1. Part of speech description.

Part of speech	Description
NN	Singular or plural noun
DT	Determiner
VB	Verb, base form
VBD	Past tense verb
IN	Preposition or subordinating conjunction
VBZ	Verb, third-person singular present
NNP	Singular proper noun
"TO"	Word "TO"
JJ	Adjective

connected dense layer with batch normalization, and an Additive Angular Margin (AAM) Softmax layer. Finally, an output layer to classify the inputs as yes or no for verification results.

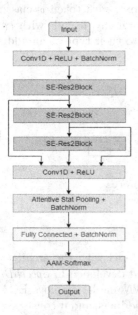

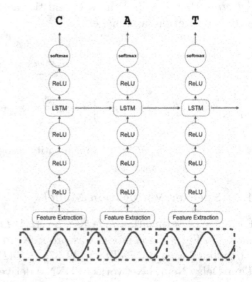

Fig. 4. ECAPA-TDNN model for speaker verification.

Fig. 5. Recurrent neural network structure of deepspeech model (https://deepspeech. readthedocs.io/en/r0.9/DeepSpeech.html).

4.3   Speech Recognition Model

We use *Deepspeech* model originally proposed by the Silicon Valley AI Lab and developed and maintained by Mozilla to convert spoken language into texts.

DeepSpeech is an end-to-end speech recognition model that utilizes *Recurrent Neural Networks (RNN)* as a type Deep Neural Networks (DNN). It also employs multi-GPU computation with optimization criteria, in addition to data synthesis mechanisms. DeepSpeech model architecture is shown in Fig. 5, it consists of a sequence of an input layer for features extraction and takes spectrograms as inputs, three hidden layers with ReLU activation, an LSTM hidden layer, another hidden layer with ReLU activation, and a final softmax output layer to generate English text transcriptions [4, 15]. Since this work is focused on investigating the privacy aspect and the effect of combining privacy mechanisms with available techniques related to speaker verification and speech recognition, we don't give further details concerning the model architecture.

4.4   Text to Speech Model

To convert anonymized text resulting from the speech recognition and sensitive entities elimination into audio files, we use *Google Text-to-Speech (gTTS)* tool[2], which is a Python library used to interface with Google Translate's text-to-speech API. It takes a text with various and unlimited lengths as inputs and converts them into voice outputs with human-like reading and intonation, in addition to precise pronunciation corrections. *gTTS* uses a wide range of voices, so that the voice of the original speaker can be replaced with any of these voices to keep the identity of the speaker anonymous.

5   Experiments

This section reports the speaker verification and speech recognition experiments performed on the Librispeech dataset[3] [31] using the privacy-preserving mechanisms described in Subsect. 4.1. The experiments are conducted to measure *data utility* after applying the privacy mechanisms represented by the similarity of the data analysis results obtained with the privacy mechanisms enforced compared to the results with no privacy enforcement and how much change is resulting from the privacy mechanisms. We are considering a use case in which local or remote data analysis can be performed with all discussed privacy mechanisms applied at the stakeholder's and server's sides depending on the shared data, and with all identified sensitive entities to be removed from the data.

The *Librispeech dataset* is a well-known dataset of audio files collected from the LibriVox project audio books. It is split into three parts for training, development, and test sets. We used the clean test set of 2, 620 audio files in our experiments to validate two pre-trained speaker verification and speech recognition models. We used 10, 000 audio files of 5, 000 pairs for matched speaker verification and 10, 000 audio files of 5, 000 pairs for mismatched speaker verification. Also, we used 2, 620 audio files from the test dataset for speech recognition.

---

[2] https://gtts.readthedocs.io/en/latest/.
[3] http://wwwopenslr.org!12/.

The speaker verification model is implemented using the *SpeechBrain* Framework[4] [32,37], specifically the ECAPA-TDNN Model. The speech recognition model is implemented using the *Deepspeech* Framework[5] based on the approach proposed in [4,15] by Mozilla. Considering the privacy perspective, a Python *Cryptography library*[6] [23] is used for data encryption and decryption using *Fernet, AES* encryption algorithm, *SHA-256*, and *HMAC*. Also, a Python *Hashlib library* is used for identity hashing[7]. Moreover, *spaCy* Python library[8] is used for Named Entity Recognition, and a Google python library *gTTS*[9] for *Text-to-Speech* is used to convert anonymized text into anonymized audio files.

5.1   Speaker Verification Experiments

We conducted the experiments for speaker verification using *ECAPA-TDNN* Model with *PLDA* by *SpeechBrain* framework. We used the weights of the pre-trained *ECAPA-TDNN model*, that has been trained on the *VoxCeleb2* standard dataset [9] and evaluated on the *VoxCeleb1* test sets [28]. The performance of the model[10] was measured by the *Equal Error Rate (EER)*, which corresponds to the error rate value when the *false acceptance error rate* is equal to the false *rejection error rate*. The *false acceptance error rate* is the rate of incorrectly accepted speaker speech segments to the total number of speech segments, while the *false rejection error rate* is the rate of incorrectly rejected speaker speech segments to the total number of speech segments. For our model, the *EER* value is equal to 0.80% which represents a higher accuracy, since the error rate is very low [32].

Referring back to the speaker verification reference scenario shown in Fig. 1, the pipeline starts first by encrypting the audio files that must be compared to verify the speaker in both files using an encryption key generated with the Python *Cryptography*. Then the encrypted files are passed to the speaker verification model, either locally or transmitted to the remote server. Trying to access the audio file without having the key fails and an error message is returned.

Moreover, speakers' identities are hashed to better protect the privacy of the users as presented in Table 2, and real user identities are removed.

Table 2. User identity protection with hashing algorithms.

Speaker ID	Speaker name	Hash
5152	Liam Neely	38c70d00164e016d42a8ba7769d07e43a4fddfceea96408ce7821081a4996fda
5132	David Stryker	5ba237d82cbbc02b959cfb31263b4ba6f8301456ae1707fc3d2524ba62bda467

---

[4] https://github.com/speechbrain/speechbrain.
[5] https://github.com/mozilla/DeepSpeech.
[6] https://cryptography.io/en/latest/.
[7] https://docs.python.org/3.5/library/hashlib.html.
[8] https://spacy.io/.
[9] https://gtts.readthedocs.io/en/latest/l.
[10] https://github.com/speechbrain/speechbrain.

Finally, the speaker verification is performed on the audio files after being decrypted and considering hashed identities instead of the real names of the speakers. Sample speaker verification results are shown in Table 4 for two audio files with different speakers and Table 3 for two audio files for the same speaker.

Table 3. Audio files with matched speaker verification.

Fields	Speaker_ID	Audio_file	Score	Prediction
First_speaker	51e862a18e2b7961382dfabd39cb41b154dead150a80e86eb63de85232e38bbc	5142-33396-0019.flac	0.709996581	True
Second_speaker	51e862a18e2b7961382dfabd39cb41b154dead150a80e86eb63de85232e38bbc	5142-33396-0022.flac		

Table 4. Audio files with mismatched speaker verification.

Fields	Speaker_ID	Audio_file	Score	Prediction
First_speaker	5ba237d82cbbc02b959cfb31263b4ba6f8301456ae1707fc3d2524ba62bda467	1995-1836-0007.flac	−0.01122827	False
Second_speaker	5ba237d82cbbc02b959cfb31263b4ba6f8301456ae1707fc3d2524ba62bda467	7176-88083-0006.flac		

We validated the speaker verification model with the use of privacy mechanisms on 10,000 audio files of 5,000 pairs for matched speaker verification, and 10,000 audio files of 5,000 pairs for mismatched speakers verification. The results of matched speaker verification show that the model has predicted 99.3% of the pairs correctly with a total number of 4,964 pairs. For mismatched speakers verification, the model has predicted 96.4% of the pairs correctly as different speakers with a total number of 4,820 pairs.

5.2 Speech Recognition Experiments

We conducted the experiments for speech recognition using *Deepspeech* Framework based on the RNN model proposed in [4,15]. We used the weights of the pre-trained model[11], that has been trained on the *LibriSpeech* train set achieves an 7.06% *Word Error Rate (WER)* on the LibriSpeech clean test set [4,15]. *WER* uses the *Levenshtein distance* metric to measure the speech recognition accuracy by comparing the original and predicted transcriptions [34].

Considering the speech recognition reference scenario shown in Fig. 2, the pipeline starts first by encrypting the audio file that must be recognized. Similar to the encryption performed in the speaker verification scenario, an encryption key is generated and the file is then passed to the speech recognition model, either locally or transmitted to a remote server. Then, the speech recognition model identifies spoken words and converts them into written transcripts. We used the *Librispeech* clean test set of 2,620 audio files for speech recognition model validation, and we used the *cosine similarity* metric shown in Eq. 1 to measure the similarity between the original speech data and the recognized text to quantify the data utility of the texts, where W and M are the two multidimensional representation vectors of n total number of vector items, with output

---

[11] https://github.com/mozilla/DeepSpeech.

similarity value in the range $[-1, +1]$ [29]. Figure 6 shows the similarity percentage categorized in 11 categories in the legend box, and for each category, the percentage of the audio files that fall under this category out of the total number of files. According to the figure, 27.2% of the files were fully correctly recognized by the model, 75% of the audio files were recognized with more than 90% similarity with the speech data, and 89.2% of the audio files were recognized with more than 80% similarity with the speech data.

$$cos(W, M) = \frac{\sum_{i=0}^{n} W_i M_i}{\sum_{i=0}^{n} W_i^2 \sum_{i=0}^{n} M_i^2} \tag{1}$$

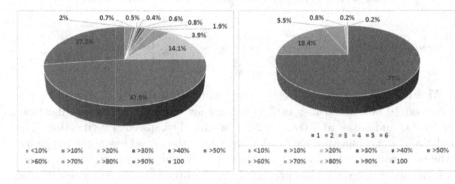

Fig. 6. Original speech to recognized speech similarity percentage.

Fig. 7. Removed sensitive phrases count-percentage.

We used the *spaCy* python library to perform entity recognition on the text recognized from the previous step. For this, we have defined the presented entities in Table 5 as the sensitive entities to be removed from the text, and this list of entities can be edited based on the user's privacy preference. Once these entities are identified in the text, our method removes and replaces them with the phrase *"Private Data"* like in the sample shown in Table 6.

For the whole test set with 2, 620 audio files, only 635 files included sensitive private entities. Figure 7 shows the count of sensitive entities removed from the text added to the legend and the percentage of modified files per modifications count plotted. It can be observed from the figure that 75% of the modified files had only one private entity removed from the text, and 18.4% had two private entities removed. We can conclude from this, that the dataset does not include highly sensitive and private attributes.

Figure 8 shows the similarity percentage categorized in 10 categories in the legend box, and for each category, the percentage of the audio files that fall under this category out of the total number of files. According to the figure, 54.8% of the audio files were anonymized with more than 90% similarity with the recognized data, 80.5% of the audio files were anonymized with more than 80% similarity

Table 5. Names and description of sensitive entities detected by spaCy [38]

Entity	Description
PERSON	People, including fictional
NORP	Nationalities or religious or political groups
FAC	Buildings, airports, highways, bridges, etc.
ORG	Companies, agencies, institutions, etc.
GPE	Countries, cities, states
LOC	Non-GPE locations, mountain ranges, bodies of water
PRODUCT	Objects, vehicles, foods, etc. (Not services.)
EVENT	Named hurricanes, battles, wars, sports events, etc.
WORK_OF_ART	Titles of books, songs, etc.
LAW	Named documents made into laws
LANGUAGE	Any named language
DATE	Absolute or relative dates or periods
TIME	Times smaller than a day
PERCENT	Percentage, including "%"
MONEY	Monetary values, including unit
QUANTITY	Measurements, as of weight or distance
ORDINAL	"first", "second", etc.
CARDINAL	Numerals that do not fall under another type

Table 6. Recognition and anonymization sample

Speech data	ruth sat quite still for a time with face intent and flushed it was out now
Recognized text	ruth sat quite still for a time with face intent and flushed it was out now
Anonymized text	Private Data sat quite still for a time with face intent and flushed it was out now

with the recognized data, and 90.2% of the audio files were anonymized with more than 70% similarity with the recognized data.

After generating anonymous texts, we use *gTTS* library to anonymize the original speaker's voice and produce a new audio file using the anonymous text with an anonymous voice, so that the identity of the speaker and sensitive information remains confidential. Finally, the anonymous text and the anonymous audio file are encrypted with the shared key and stored locally if the analysis is performed on the user side or shared again with the user if it is done remotely.

5.3   Results Discussion

We investigated the effect of applying privacy mechanisms for data encryption, hashing, and anonymization on the *Data Utility* and *Results Accuracy* for Speaker Verification and Speech Recognition in two architectures for local and

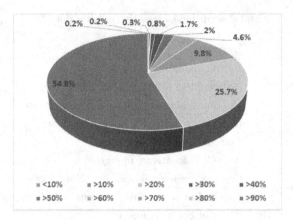

Fig. 8. Recognized speech to anonymized speech similarity percentage.

remote data analysis. In the first classification scenario investigated in our experiments, which is the privacy-preserving speaker verification, we applied identity hashing in addition to file encryption privacy mechanisms without modifying the original files. We found out that the accuracy of the results was very high in the case of matched speaker verification with 99.3% accuracy and in the case of mismatched speaker verification with 96.4% accuracy.

Moreover, we have studied the impact of the privacy mechanism on the second scenario, where privacy-preserving speech recognition is performed. We used encryption, hashing, anonymization, and speaker voice replacement to protect the privacy of individuals. Encryption and hashing have no impact on the data utility like in the previous scenario. However, data anonymization has a limited impact on the similarity of the produced text by the speech recognition model with more than 90% of the anonymized data being similar with at least 70% and more the 54% with more than 90% similarity. Therefore, *Data Utility* is minimally affected by the adoption of the anonymization privacy mechanism that can be controlled by the sensitive entities the user select.

However, our methodology provides a mechanism for continuous speaker verification and speech recognition together for related contexts such as online examination or conversational systems, in which user identity must be verified and the data must be recognized and remain private, and can also be used as separate solutions where the user identity, biometric information, and data are protected with a limited impact on the results accuracy and data utility.

6   Conclusion and Future Work

Concerns related to users' privacy are arising in recent years, especially with the great advances in smart environments and biometric data analysis techniques with the possibility to perform these analysis operations remotely. In this paper, we have proposed an approach for a secure and privacy-preserving implementation of speaker verification and speech recognition Deep Learning models, i.e., without violating the privacy of users in local remote data analysis and considering also the results accuracy. We have ensured a privacy-preserving approach by the usage of cryptography algorithms and data anonymization.

We proposed, thus, a methodology based on two deep learning-based approaches for audio datasets analysis, which preserves data privacy and archives accurate data analysis results. The experiments demonstrated the validity of our approach and how it is possible to get accurate data analysis results with no privacy violation. As a future extension to this work, we plan to extend the application of the privacy mechanisms to Speaker Diarization models, in which several speakers are included in the same audio file. Besides, we also plan to consider voice datasets with high sensitivity and longer audio times, so that the privacy gain and anonymization be more effective in such contexts.

References

1. Abdel-Hamid, O., Mohamed, A.R., Jiang, H., Deng, L., Penn, G., Yu, D.: Convolutional neural networks for speech recognition. IEEE/ACM Trans. Audio Speech Lang. Process. **22**(10), 1533–1545 (2014)
2. Aloufi, R., Haddadi, H., Boyle, D.: Emotionless: privacy-preserving speech analysis for voice assistants. arXiv preprint arXiv:1908.03632 (2019)
3. Amberkar, A., Awasarmol, P., Deshmukh, G., Dave, P.: Speech recognition using recurrent neural networks. In: 2018 International Conference on Current Trends Towards Converging Technologies (ICCTCT), pp. 1–4. IEEE (2018)
4. Amodei, D., et al.: Deep speech 2: end-to-end speech recognition in English and mandarin. In: International Conference on Machine Learning, pp. 173–182. PMLR (2016)
5. Barker, E.B., et al.: Secure hash standard (SHS) [includes change notice from 2/25/2004] (2002)
6. Blazhevski, D., Bozhinovski, A., Stojchevska, B., Pachovski, V.: Modes of operation of the AES algorithm (2013)
7. Bolton, T., Dargahi, T., Belguith, S., Al-Rakhami, M.S., Sodhro, A.H.: On the security and privacy challenges of virtual assistants. Sensors **21**(7), 2312 (2021)
8. Campbell, W.M., Sturim, D.E., Reynolds, D.A.: Support vector machines using GMM supervectors for speaker verification. IEEE Sig. Process. Lett. **13**(5), 308–311 (2006)
9. Chung, J.S., Nagrani, A., Zisserman, A.: VoxCeleb2: deep speaker recognition. arXiv preprint arXiv:1806.05622 (2018)
10. Cramer, R., Damgård, I.B., et al.: Secure Multiparty Computation. Cambridge University Press, Cambridge (2015)
11. Desplanques, B., Thienpondt, J., Demuynck, K.: ECAPA-TDNN: emphasized channel attention, propagation and aggregation in TDNN based speaker verification. arXiv preprint arXiv:2005.07143 (2020)
12. Dworkin, M.J., et al.: Advanced encryption standard (AES) (2001)
13. Gilad-Bachrach, R., Dowlin, N., Laine, K., Lauter, K., Naehrig, M., Wernsing, J.: CryptoNets: applying neural networks to encrypted data with high throughput and accuracy. In: International Conference on Machine Learning, pp. 201–210. PMLR (2016)

14. Graves, A., Mohamed, A.R., Hinton, G.: Speech recognition with deep recurrent neural networks. In: 2013 IEEE International Conference on Acoustics, Speech and Signal Processing, pp. 6645–6649. IEEE (2013)
15. Hannun, A., et al.: Deep speech: scaling up end-to-end speech recognition. arXiv preprint arXiv:1412.5567 (2014)
16. Heron, S.: Advanced encryption standard (AES). Netw. Secur. **2009**(12), 8–12 (2009)
17. Hosseini, H., Yun, S., Park, H., Louizos, C., Soriaga, J., Welling, M.: Federated learning of user authentication models. arXiv preprint arXiv:2007.04618 (2020)
18. Huang, K., Liu, X., Fu, S., Guo, D., Xu, M.: A lightweight privacy-preserving CNN feature extraction framework for mobile sensing. IEEE Trans. Dependable Secure Comput. **18**(3), 1441–1455 (2019)
19. Juang, B.H., Rabiner, L.R.: Hidden Markov models for speech recognition. Technometrics **33**(3), 251–272 (1991)
20. Kenny, P.: Bayesian speaker verification with, heavy tailed priors. In: Proceedings of Odyssey 2010 (2010)
21. Krawczyk, H., Bellare, M., Canetti, R.: HMAC: keyed-hashing for message authentication. Technical report (1997)
22. Kröger, J.L., Gellrich, L., Pape, S., Brause, S.R., Ullrich, S.: Personal information inference from voice recordings: user awareness and privacy concerns. Proc. Priv. Enhancing Technol. **2022**(1), 6–27 (2022)
23. Kuchling, A.: Python cryptography toolkit. Release **2**(1), 1–16 (2008)
24. Liu, J., Juuti, M., Lu, Y., Asokan, N.: Oblivious neural network predictions via minionn transformations. In: Proceedings of the 2017 ACM SIGSAC Conference on Computer and Communications Security, pp. 619–631 (2017)
25. Malik, M., Malik, M.K., Mehmood, K., Makhdoom, I.: Automatic speech recognition: a survey. Multimed. Tools Appl. **80**(6), 9411–9457 (2021). https://doi.org/10.1007/s11042-020-10073-7
26. McLaren, M., Lawson, A., Lei, Y., Scheffer, N.: Adaptive Gaussian backend for robust language identification. In: Interspeech, pp. 84–88 (2013)
27. Mohit, B.: Named entity recognition. In: Zitouni, I. (ed.) Natural Language Processing of Semitic Languages. TANLP, pp. 221–245. Springer, Heidelberg (2014). https://doi.org/10.1007/978-3-642-45358-8_7
28. Nagrani, A., Chung, J.S., Zisserman, A.: VoxCeleb: a large-scale speaker identification dataset. arXiv preprint arXiv:1706.08612 (2017)
29. Nguyen, H.V., Bai, L.: Cosine similarity metric learning for face verification. In: Kimmel, R., Klette, R., Sugimoto, A. (eds.) ACCV 2010. LNCS, vol. 6493, pp. 709–720. Springer, Heidelberg (2011). https://doi.org/10.1007/978-3-642-19309-5_55
30. Paar, C., Pelzl, J.: Understanding Cryptography: A Textbook for Students and Practitioners. Springer, Heidelberg (2009). https://doi.org/10.1007/978-3-642-04101-3
31. Panayotov, V., Chen, G., Povey, D., Khudanpur, S.: LibriSpeech: an ASR corpus based on public domain audio books. In: 2015 IEEE International Conference on Acoustics, Speech and Signal Processing (ICASSP), pp. 5206–5210. IEEE (2015)
32. Parcollet, T., et al.: SpeechBrain: a general-purpose speech toolkit (2022)
33. Pathak, M.A., Raj, B.: Privacy-preserving speaker verification and identification using gaussian mixture models. IEEE Trans. Audio Speech Lang. Process. **21**(2), 397–406 (2012)
34. Po, D.K.: Similarity based information retrieval using Levenshtein distance algorithm. Int. J. Adv. Sci. Res. Eng. **6**(04), 06–10 (2020)

35. Qian, J., et al.: VoiceMask: anonymize and sanitize voice input on mobile devices. arXiv preprint arXiv:1711.11460 (2017)
36. Rahulamathavan, Y.: Privacy-preserving similarity calculation of speaker features using fully homomorphic encryption. arXiv preprint arXiv:2202.07994 (2022)
37. Ravanelli, M., et al.: SpeechBrain: a general-purpose speech toolkit. arXiv preprint arXiv:2106.04624 (2021)
38. Room, C.: Named entity recognition. Algorithms 8(3), 48 (2020)
39. Safavi, S., Russell, M., Jančovič, P.: Automatic speaker, age-group and gender identification from children's speech. Comput. Speech Lang. 50, 141–156 (2018)
40. Schuller, B., Batliner, A.: Computational Paralinguistics: Emotion, Affect and Personality in Speech and Language Processing. Wiley, Hoboken (2013)
41. Schuller, B., Rigoll, G., Lang, M.: Hidden Markov model-based speech emotion recognition. In: 2003 IEEE International Conference on Acoustics, Speech, and Signal Processing, Proceedings (ICASSP 2003), vol. 2, pp. II-1. IEEE (2003)
42. Swietojanski, P., Ghoshal, A., Renals, S.: Convolutional neural networks for distant speech recognition. IEEE Sig. Process. Lett. 21(9), 1120–1124 (2014)
43. Tan, C.B., Hijazi, M.H.A., Khamis, N., Zainol, Z., Coenen, F., Gani, A., et al.: A survey on presentation attack detection for automatic speaker verification systems: state-of-the-art, taxonomy, issues and future direction. Multimed. Tools nd Appl. 80(21), 32725–32762 (2021). https://doi.org/10.1007/s11042-021-11235-x
44. Treiber, A., Nautsch, A., Kolberg, J., Schneider, T., Busch, C.: Privacy-preserving PLDA speaker verification using outsourced secure computation. Speech Commun. 114, 60–71 (2019)
45. Vaidya, T., Sherr, M.: You talk too much: limiting privacy exposure via voice input. In: 2019 IEEE Security and Privacy Workshops (SPW), pp. 84–91. IEEE (2019)
46. Yi, X., Paulet, R., Bertino, E.: Homomorphic encryption. In: Yi, X., Paulet, R., Bertino, E. (eds.) Homomorphic Encryption and Applications. SCS, pp. 27–46. Springer, Cham (2014). https://doi.org/10.1007/978-3-319-12229-8_2

An E-Voting System Based on Tornado Cash

Stefano Bistarelli, Bruno Lazo La Torre Montalvo, Ivan Mercanti[(✉)],
and Francesco Santini

Department of Maths and Computer Science, University of Perugia, Perugia, Italy
{stefano.bistarelli,bruno.montalvo,ivan.mercanti,
francesco.santini}@unipg.it

Abstract. We propose an pseudo-anonymous e-voting platform based on
the blockchain of Ethereum and a coin-mixer, that is Tornado Cash. After
an online authentication and authorization phase, the user receives a fungible (i.e., pseudo-anonymous) voting token that can be deposited to a
coin pool belonging to Tornado Cash (TC), together with an amount of
Ether (ETH) A that will be used to pay successive fees. TC uses a smart
contract that accepts token deposits that can be later withdrawn by a different address. In order to preserve privacy, a *relayer* contract can then
be used to withdraw to a fresh ETH address (thus pseudo-anonymous)
using A to pay fees. Relayers solve "fee payment dilemma", that is paying withdrawal fees by maintaining pseudo-anonymity. Finally, a further
smart contract collects preferences and, after the closure of the elections,
it automatically performs the counting of votes. All the front-end has been
developed in a Web browser, by using Javascript and avoiding the voter
to perform any command-line operation to prepare transactions.

Keywords: E-voting · Ethereum · Anonymity

1 Introduction

The right to vote is one of the most important forms of manifestation of personal freedom and democratic expression. Thanks to the right to vote, citizens
have the opportunity to intervene in important decisions for the collectivity:
it is therefore important that this right is exercised freely, secretly and with a
wide opportunity of choice. E-voting (or electronic voting) refers to the use of
electronic and computer technologies during the voting or counting process. As
a first important observation, we would like to remark that the e-voting system
we propose in this paper is not anyway considered as a substitute of traditional
voting systems based on paper ballots, in election scenarios that support rep-
resentative democracy in local, regional or national governments. We instead
support the use of e-voting systems in case the application is less sensitive and
attracts less interest in being massively attacked, thus invalidating the electoral
process and causing disorder. For example, we think of elections concerning the
administrative councils and boards of organizations and companies, especially
those ones decentralized around the world.

© Springer Nature Switzerland AG 2023
A. Saracino and P. Mori (Eds.): ETAA 2022, LNCS 13782, pp. 120–135, 2023.
https://doi.org/10.1007/978-3-031-25467-3_8

Our favourite scenario for the e-voting system we propose consists of tens/hundreds voters (but not millions) who want/need to remain pseudo-anonymous, who can spend a few euro to vote, who cannot meet in presence, but need strong guarantees on the security and privacy of the elections result. Such warrants are in this case offered by a blockchain-based system, which we will explain in the following of the paper.

Some issues associated with "traditional" voting systems that uses paper ballots are represented by: their high cost derived from the use of equipment (for voting operations, tellers, polling chairmen); the time (in days) that can pass from the time the voting operation is completed to the time the count results are published; the low accessibility: statistically, having to physically reach the seat of the polling station is one of the major causes of voting abstention. The use of e-voting can mitigate these drawbacks, since the cost is in general lower, the voting operation results in an immediate counting (with no human error), a mobile device is enough to cast a preference vote from anywhere and, finally, filling in the ballot is guided through mouse clicks, thus eliminating null votes due to errors in filling in the ballot paper.

The purpose of this study is the implementation of an electronic voting system based on blockchain technology, which satisfies some classical properties of an e-voting system (see Sect. 2.3). For the implementation of such a system the following objectives have been identified: *i)* the distribution of a fungible ERC20 token dedicated to voting: we implemented the entire system within the Ethereum blockchain, creating a token that is distributed to an authorized user after identification. *ii)* User pseudo-anonymization: we implemented (readapting it from an existing solution, not oriented to e-voting) a coin-mixing service that allows a user to carry out deposit and withdrawal of the voting token in a decentralized and privacy-oriented manner. Finally, *iii)* the system is offered through a decentralized application (or *dApp*) dedicated to voting: we designed a dApp that allows the user to cast his vote by spending his voting token.

The application we propose in this paper elaborates on the Tornado Cash smart contract, which improves transaction privacy by breaking the on-chain link between source and destination addresses. This contract accepts ETH deposits that can be withdrawn by a different address. In order to preserve privacy, a *relayer* can be used to withdraw to an address with no ETH balance (i.e., a fresh address). Whenever ETH is withdrawn by the new address, there is no way to link the withdrawal to the deposit, ensuring complete privacy. Tornado Cash originally proposes itself as a coin-mixer service: these tools are intended to mix digital money with that of other users in order to obfuscate the source and destination of crypto assets. It is here used as a way to preserve pseudo-anonymity of preference votes.

The front-end of the application has been developed in Javascript, so that the user can easily perform all the operations by using a plain Web-browser, without interacting with the Ethereum blockchain with (more complicated) command-line tools.

The paper is organized as follows. Section 2 contains an overview of Ethereum, ERC20 Tornado Cash and e-voting system. Our e-voting model is presented in Sect. 3. Section 4 compares our proposal with other works in the literature and Sect. 5 draws some conclusions and discusses possible future work.

2 Background

In this section we partition the necessary background information to later describe how our e-voting proposal based on the blockchain of Ethereum works. First of all, Sect. 2.1 briefly introduces Ethereum, while Sect. 2.2 presents the main token standard in Ethereum, i.e., ERC20. Then we list the most important properties that a voting system should satisfy in Sect. 2.3. Finally, Tornado Cash is presented in Sect. 2.4.

2.1   Ethereum

Ethereum is a blockchain protocol created by Vitalik Buterin [5], which implements different features respect to the Bitcoin protocol. The main feature, which made it popular and second only to Bitcoin in terms of volume, is the possibility to create decentralized apps (*dApps*) via smart contracts.

Smart contracts are programs based on rule sets and deployed on the Ethereum blockchain, which allows functions to be executed if certain conditions are met.[1] Ethereum smart contracts can be written using several programming Turing-equivalent languages, but the most popular is Solidity created by Gavin Wood, one of Ethereum's co-founders. These contracts can execute transactions automatically, so there is no need for a third-party entity to take action.

dApps are in general applications that connects a smart contract with a front-end user interface.[2] To be defined as dApp, an application needs to be:

– *Decentralized*: operating within the blockchain, where no entity has control.
– *Deterministic*: a certain input always correspond to the same output.
– *Turing-complete*: every action can be performed with the required resource.
– *Isolated*: executing on a virtual environment called Ethereum Virtual Machine (EVM), so, in case of failure, the blockchain network will not be affected.

2.2   The ERC20 Standard

ERC-20 is the technical standard for fungible tokens created using the Ethereum blockchain. A fungible token is interchangeable with another token, while the well-known non-fungible tokens (NFTs) are not interchangeable.[3] ERC-20 offers

---

[1] Smart contracts: https://github.com/ethereum/ethereum-org-website/blob/dev/sr c/content/developers/docs/smart-contracts/index.md.
[2] dApps: https://github.com/ethereum/ethereum-org-website/blob/dev/src/conten t/developers/docs/dapps/index.md.
[3] https://www.investopedia.com/news/what-erc20-and-what-does-it-mean-ether eum/.

several functions and events that a token must implement. The minimum of functions and information needed in an ERC-20 compliant token is:

- *TotalSupply*: the total number of tokens that will ever be issued.
- *BalanceOf*: the account balance of a token owner's account.
- *Transfer*: automatically executes transfers of a specified number of tokens to a specified address for transactions using the token.
- *TransferFrom*: automatically executes transfers of a specified number of tokens from a specified address using the token.
- *Approve*: allows a spender to withdraw a set number of tokens from a specified account, up to a specific amount.
- *Allowance*: returns the remaining number of tokens that spender will be allowed to spend on behalf of owner.
- *Transfer*: an event triggered when a transfer is successful.
- *Approval*: a log of an approved event.

2.3 Important Voting Properties

A good voting (and also e-voting) system has to satisfy the following properties [6,10,14], in particular:

- *Verifiability*: it is possible to verify that the counting of votes has been performed correctly.
- *Uniqueness*: a user is not allowed to vote more than once.
- *Integrity*: no one can change or delete a vote without revealing it.
- *Privacy*: it is not possible to determine the vote of a user.
- *Counting*: the vote count has to be verifiable by everyone.
- *Authentication*: only users who have correctly identified themselves can vote.
- *Confidentiality*: intermediate results cannot be obtained during the proceedings.
- *Lack of evidence*: users cannot prove for whom they voted.
- *Reliability*: the voting system must be reliable and stable.

2.4 Tornado Cash

Tornado Cash is an open-source, fully decentralized non-custodial[4] protocol implemented within the Ethereum blockchain. It improves transaction privacy by breaking the on-chain link between source and destination addresses. It uses a smart contract that accepts ether and other ERC20 tokens deposits from one address and enables their withdrawal from a different address. Tornado Cash smart contracts are implemented on the Ethereum blockchain, so they can

---

[4] Non-custodial wallet services are platforms that allow users to possess their private keys.

neither be modified nor tampered with. Mining smart contracts and administration smart contracts are implemented by the community in a decentralized way: any user can propose a smart contract and anyone can vote for or against it by locking *TORN*s (i.e., *Tornado Cash tokens*). After 5 days, if a minimum of 25000 TORNs has been reached and the proposal is voted by the majority of votes, it is approved. Hence, it changes the mining and the administration smart contracts.

Tornado Cash is currently operating with several different cryptocurrencies and layer-2 networks:

- Ethereum Blockchain: ETH (Ethereum), DAI (Dai), cDAI (Compound Dai), USDC (USD Coin), USDT (Tether) & WBTC (Wrapped Bitcoin),
- Binance Smart Chain: BNB (Binance Coin),
- Polygon Network: MATIC (Polygon),
- Gnosis Chain (former xDAI Chain): xDAI (xDai),
- Avalanche Mainnet: AVAX (Avalanche),
- Optimism, as a Layer-2 for ETH (Ethereum),
- Arbitrum One, as a Layer-2 ETH (Ethereum).

The user who wants to make a deposit[5] in the pool, will have to randomly generate a *secret k* and a *nullifier r* with $k, r \in \mathbb{B}^{248}$, and its hash called *commitment C*, such that $C = H_1(k||r)$.[6] Along with N tokens are then sent to the smart contract $\mathcal{C}$ interpreting C as a 256-bit unsigned integer. The contract will then accept the deposit of the N token and add C as a leaf of a tree, in case the tree is not full.[7]

To withdraw (Fig. 1), the user must select the recipient's address A with a transaction fee f such that $f \leq N$. Then, the user should provide proof that he/she possesses a secret to an unspent commitment from the smart contract's list of deposits. The *zkSnark*[8] technology allows doing that without revealing which exact deposit corresponds to this secret. The smart contract will check the proof, and transfer deposited funds to the address specified for withdrawal. An external observer will be unable to determine which deposit this withdrawal comes from.

To perform the withdrawal, two different options are available:

- The user links their wallet (*Metamask* or *WalletConnect*) to the Tornado Cash website, and they pay for the gas needed to withdraw the amount deposited.
- The user use a *relayer* to make the withdrawal to any Ethereum address without needing to make the wallet connection on the Tornado Cash website.

---

[5] Web-connection of Tornado Cash to Metamask or a private wallet: https://tornadocash.eth.limo/.

[6] With || that stands for concatenation.

[7] https://tornado-cash.medium.com/introducing-private-transactions-on-ethereum-now-42ee915babe0.

[8] zk-SNARK: https://z.cash/technology/zksnarks/.

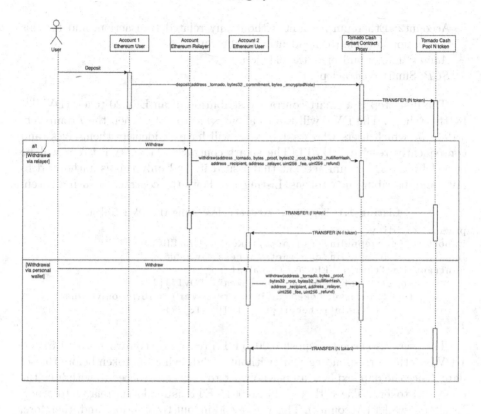

Fig. 1. Sequence diagram: deposit and withdrawal operations.

Since the relayer is in charge of paying for the transaction gas, it will receive a small portion of the deposit.

The user's deposit and withdrawal actions are performed by interacting with the smart contract of the Tornado Cash Proxy.[9]

3   The E-Voting Model

We aim to design an e-voting model that satisfies the properties described in Sect. 2.3. Moreover, we want to achieve three other goals: the token distribution, the user pseudo-anonymization and the voting dApp distribution. To better understand our model, in this section we refer to the various actors as follows:

- *Account1*: Ethereum account with ether and possibly other tokens. Not anonymous, linked to a voter.

---

[9] Goerli Testnet Network: https://goerli.etherscan.io/address/0x454d870a72e29d5e 5697f635128d18077bd04c60.

- Account2: Ethereum account without any related transaction, and for this reason not linkable to the identity of the voter.
- *Admin*: The organizer of the election.
- *SCP*: Smart contract pool.

The first step is a smart contract distribution of an ERC20 token (DVT[10]) by the Admin. The DVT will use to allow users to vote. Then the Admin sets a date by which users who want to vote will have to identify themselves (and consequently receive 1 DVT). The smart contract of the DVT token will be owned by the Ethereum account that issued it, and only this is authorized to mint and distribute new tokens. Listing 1.1 shows the contract of such a token.

Listing 1.1. The smart contract describing the DVT Token

```
pragma solidity ^0.8.0;
import "@openzeppelin/contracts/token/ERC20/ERC20.sol ";
import "@openzeppelin/contracts/access/Ownable.sol ";
contract DevToken is ERC20, Ownable{
        constructor() ERC20("DevToken", "DVT"){}
        function issueToken(address receiver) public onlyOwner{
            _mint( receiver , 1*10**18); }
}
```

The users also need to deposit 0.0015 ETH (currently equivalent to €1.5) and 1 DVT to the corresponding SCP, without withdrawing the token before the set date. Once the date expires, users who want to vote can proceed to withdraw the deposited tokens. The withdrawal of 0.0015 ETH is made via relayer to a new Ethereum wallet (Account2). This is to avoid in/out transactions and, therefore, to pseudo-anonymize the user. The user withdraws 1 DTV on the same wallet (Account2). Finally, the Admin makes public the dApp websites allowing users to vote by sending the DVT token to the smart contract dedicated to voting.

Figure 2 shows how the distribution of a token works. The Admin creates a smart contract. The smart contract implementation of a new ERC20 token (DVT) is used to secure voting rights. It is deployed on the Goerli test network (or briefly *testnet*) via the Hardhat[11] development environment. The smart contract is owned by the Ethereum account that released it (Admin), and only that account will be able to generate new tokens. It is possible to control from the smart contract the number of tokens in circulation and the Ethereum accounts that own them. Admin also authenticates the user and then gives one DTV token to them. To authenticate users, Admin creates a web page with a form. The user fills this form with their personal data. Admin checks that the data are valid and the user did not already receive the DTV token. If everything is correct, the user is authenticated and receives 1 DTV token. Due to its decentralized nature, it is possible to control from the smart contract the number of coined tokens and the Ethereum accounts that own them.

---

[10] DevToken.
[11] https://hardhat.org/.

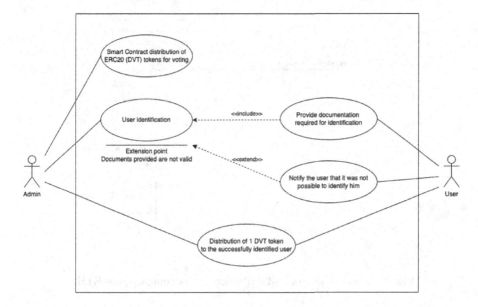

Fig. 2. Use case diagram: distribution of a vote token.

To ensure the pseudo-anonymization of users we extend in our Smart Contract the Tornado Cash protocol. In particular, we implement the deposit and withdrawal of ETH and DTV via relayer. Figure 3 and Fig. 4 describe the Sequence diagram of the tokens distribution via relayer. By executing the instructions in these figures, the SCP distributes: *i)* the smart contract hasher, which calculates the hash when a deposit is made (*2_deploy_hasher.js*), *ii)* the smart contract verifier, which verifies that the withdrawal proof is valid (*running 3_deploy_verifier.js*), *iii)* the ETH or DTV SCP using *4_deploy_eth_tornado.js* and *5_deploy_erc20_tornado.js* respectively. The Admin distributes SCP to deposit and withdraw ETH and DTV. Moreover, the SCP allows the users to deposit from Account1 and withdraw in Account2. So the user has to use SCP for deposit and withdraw operations before voting to remain pseudo-anonymous.

The user, after finalizing the deposit, receives in output a private note that they necessarily have to memorize in order to later withdraw the deposit. As has already been described, Admin sets an expiration date for making deposits. Once this date expired, the voter withdraws ETH from Account2. To pay the fee for this transaction they can not use Account1 (if the user does so, this would create a correlation between Account1 and Account2, and thus pseudo-anonymity would be lost) nor Account2 (this one does not have any ether). An Ethereum account called *relayer*, configured by the Admin, is necessary to pay the fee for an ETH withdrawal transaction. To configure the relayer, we refer to Tornado Cash's *tornado-relayer* repository on GitHub[12]. In particular, we

---

[12] https://github.com/tornadocash/tornado-relayer/tree/c838316436a9f87f8655087c3 4764b46e4b1491b.

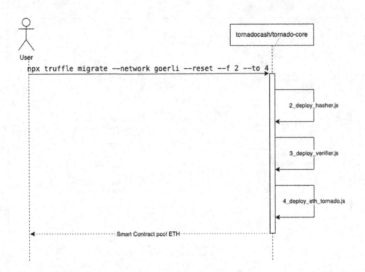

Fig. 3. Sequence diagram: distribution smart contract pool ETH.

extend it with the possibility of operating in Goerli with our SCP and to modify the transaction gas and fee value.

Figure 5 shows what a user can do with our SCP. The user can deposit either ETH or DTV from a wallet and get it in a relayer wallet in order to break their connection with the coin, i.e. with the purpose to pseudo-anonymize the user. The withdrawal function:

WITHDRAW (BYTES _PROOF, BYTES32 _ROOT,
BYTES32 _NULLIFIERHASH, ADDRESS _RECIPIENT, ADDRESS _RELAYER,
UINT256 _FEE, UINT256 _REFUND)

Where we have the recipient's address (parameter _recipient), a transaction fee (parameter _fee), the proof (parameter _proof) to make a withdrawal, a root (parameter _root) selected from those stored on the contract and the hash of the nullifier (parameter _nullifierHash).

Having performed the withdrawal transaction, the user has 0.0015 ETH and 1 DTV in their Account2. ETH value is for pay transaction fees and the DVT, instead, is for voting. At this point, the admin creates a web dApp based on smart contract. The contract can be created using the constructor:

CONSTRUCTOR(STRING[] MEMORY PROPOSALNAMES, UINT256 TOKENQUAN-
TITY_, ADDRESS TOKEN)

The smart contract constructor uses:

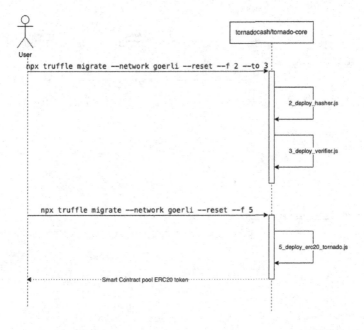

Fig. 4. Sequence diagram: distribution smart contract pool (ERC20).

- the PROPOSALNAMES parameter to set up a dynamic array that will contain the names of the candidates on the ballots;
- the TOKENQUANTITY_ parameter to set the amount of tokens needed for each user to be able to vote;
- the TOKEN parameter to indicate the address of the ERC20 token that will be required to vote.

Instead, to handle voting in the smart contract, function VOTE(UINT PROPOSAL) is used. The PROPOSAL parameter indicates the candidate selected by the voting user.

Finally, the Admin implements a web application that interacts with the smart contract of voting (Fig. 6). The user who wants to vote has to log in to their Metamask account (connected to Account2) from its extension on a browser. Then the user can access the dedicated voting web page indicated by the administrator. When this page loads, Metamask will ask the user for the smart contract permission to receive 1 DVT token from the user's wallet (GETVOTES() function in Fig. 6). Notice that it is possible only if the token is present in the user's wallet (Account2) and the user wants to vote. Finally, the user needs to wait a few seconds for the transaction to be mined on the Blockchain. Afterwards, the user can select the candidate they wish to vote for from the drop-down menu. After clicking on the button that says "Vote", Metamask will prompt the user for confirmation to call the VOTE(UINT PROPOSAL) function of the smart contract. Once this transaction is mined, the vote count received by the selected candidate will be increased.

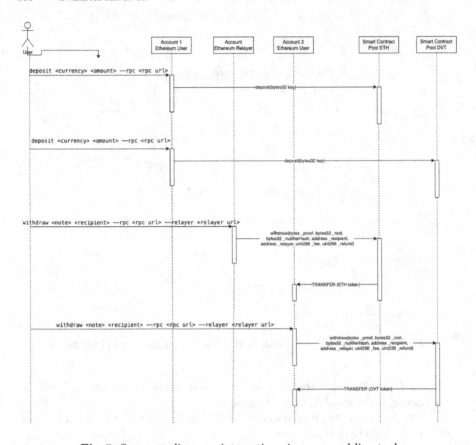

Fig. 5. Sequence diagram: interaction via command line tool.

3.1   Satisfied Properties

The proposed model satisfy the properties presented in Sect. 2.3 except for *Confidentiality* and *Lack of evidence*.

Verifiability: Transactions in the Ethereum blockchain are public, so it is always possible to verify that the counting of votes has been performed correctly.

Uniqueness: Double-voting is prevented by the fact that double-spending is not possible with the blockchain technology [5].

Integrity: When a transaction is in a confirmed block, to modify that block is computationally hard by design [5], since it is required to also modify all the successive blocks. Moreover, it is not possible to change or delete a transaction (vote) without revealing it.

Privacy: Voters' Account2 cannot be associated with their identity because the *Token Distribution* is implemented via relayer using the Tornado Cash protocol. In this way, the users have an Ethereum account without any transaction; therefore, it is not possible to identify the voter.

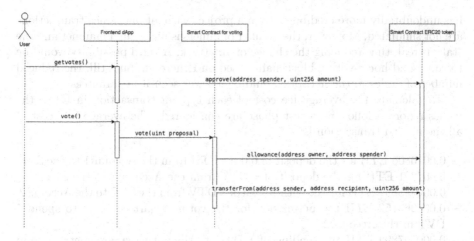

Fig. 6. Sequence diagram: user voting.

Counting: Each valid transaction is permanently stored in the blockchain, where it is possible to repeat the counting phase when needed. Any Ethereum node can repeat this phase as needed.

Authentication: This is accomplished by the authentication phase, when the Admin distributes the DTV tokens to the authenticated users.

Confidentiality: Unfortunately, this property is not satisfied by our implementation: in fact, by checking the candidates' accounts it is possible to read intermediate results.

Lack of evidence: Users, revealing the possess of their Account2, can prove for whom they voted. This means we cannot satisfy this property.

Reliability: Clearly, the reliability properties depends on many factors and it is not easy to be measured (e.g., with a simulation). However, Ethereum already proves to be a reliable and largely used infrastructure. Indeed, it is required to use transactions with a high fee in order not to lose votes; nevertheless, a voter can check if their votes has been included in the blockchain. Clearly, the size of the peer-to-peer network and the number of miners mitigate such problems.

3.2   Cost Estimation

In this section, we provide an estimation of the costs needed to cast a vote on the *Mainnet* of Ethereum. Alternatively, a public testnet can be used where ETH has no real value; the testnet used in this paper, for example, i.e., Goerli, is a *proof-of-authority* (PoA) Ethereum testnet.[13] However, a project with a mainnet

---

[13] The PoA is a consensus method that gives a small and designated number of blockchain actors the power to validate transactions or interactions with the network and to update its registry. Goerli is said to switch to proof-of-stake soon.

has undoubtedly more credibility than a project without one, since transactions are not simulated. Moreover, the number of miners is higher in a mainnet and the stake is real, thus reducing the chance of an attack. A third possibility would be to run an ad-hoc e-voting blockchain based on Ethereum, but still, the reduced number of nodes in the network would offer fewer security guarantees.

To calculate the average fee cost of each type of transaction in ETH, the values reported following a test phase are considered. The average fees cost of all the needed transaction is:

- 0.0010805 ETH for the deposit of 0.0015 ETH from the Account1 to the SCP.
- 0.001291 ETH for the deposit of 1 DTV from the Account1 to the SCP.
- 0.000448857 ETH for the withdrawal of 1 DTV from the SCP to the Account2.
- 0.000063152 ETH the permission for the voting smart contract to spend 1 DVT in the Account2.
- 0.000107894 ETH the sending of 1 DTV to the voting smart contract from the Account2 to execute the voting.

To sum up, the Account1 spend in mean 0.0023715 ETH, the Account2, instead 0.000512009 ETH. The total result is 0.0028835 ETH, around €4.20 at the time of writing.[14]

4   Related Work

Nowadays, the most spread voting schemes consists in paper-based elections. However, paper-based systems are not completely secure and they may suffer from frauds, even in today's democratic countries,[15] where controversies are very frequent.[16] Estonia became the first nation to hold general elections over the Internet with a pilot project for the municipal elections in 2005. The e-voting system withstood the test of reality and was declared a success by Estonian election officials [2]. Despite this, e-voting systems have not experienced a breakthrough in Europe, since most of the diffidence resides in the general level of trust in government, but also the level of trust in the corporations that supply the machines use in the electoral process [8].

Some proposals have been already opened in the direction outlined by this paper. The most noticeable reference is the *Bitcongress.org project*,[17] which already offers a voting platform based on Bitcoin. However, the software is offered as a broker between the voter and Bitcoin. An evidence is the presence of a "Smart Contract Blockchain": quoting the project white-paper, *"A vote token is sent by a legislation creation tool with combined cryptocurrency wallet. The vote is sent to a smart contract based election holding yay, nay and candidate addresses"*. On the contrary, in our implementation a vote is directly sent to the

---

[14] Using gas price to compute fees on 23rd of July 2022.

[15] http://news.bbc.co.uk/2/hi/uk_news/4410743.stm.

[16] http://news.bbc.co.uk/2/hi/europe/4904294.stm.

[17] Web-site of the Bitcongress.org project: http://www.bitcongress.org.

address of a candidate, without any intermediary. Moreover, still quoting the white-paper, *"The election logs then changes, the vote count is recorded and displayed within Axiomity (a decentralised application) using Bitcongress onto the Smart Contract Blockchain"*. In our solution the counting is directly performed in the blockchain. Other commercial systems are *Follow my vote*[18] and *TIVI*[19].

Envisioning the use of blockchains for voting purposes has been already proposed in [11,12,16] for example. In the following we present related scientific works. All of them propose solutions without the help of coloured coins or permissioned ledgers, which have been use to respectively simplify the counting process and satisfy further properties, as shown in Sect. 2.3: properties as data confidentiality and uncoercibility seem not be addressed in all such proposals; with *MultiChain*,[20] or in general permissioned ledgers, it is possible instead. The proposal in [3] simply consists in an electronic voting system based on the Bitcoin block-chain technology.

In [1,7] the author propose an e-voting scheme, which is then implemented in the Ethereum blockchain. The implementation and related performance measurements are given in the paper along with the challenges presented by the blockchain platform to develop a complex application like e-voting. In general, special attention must be paid to the debugging and verification steps on (Ethereum) smart-contracts. In [13] the authors show as a blockchain-based e-voting system with Ethereum and Metamask can serve as a solution to security and trust issues in the e-voting system.

Even the execution of the protocol in [9] is enforced by using the consensus mechanism that also secures the Ethereum blockchain. However, by using a permissionless blockchain, public verifiability does not provide any coercion resistance.

5   Conclusion

This study describes the process of creating an e-voting system based on the Ethereum blockchain, using the protocol implemented by the Tornado Cash coin-mixer to ensure the privacy of the voter and via smart contracts to ensure the transparency of the entire process.

First, we developed a Web application authenticating the user and subsequently distributing an ERC20 token which represents a vote. Following this, by referring to the Tornado Cash protocol: *i)* we developed smart contract pools with the purpose to allow the deposit and withdrawal of the voting tokens (DVT) and ETH, *ii)* we implemented an application through which the user can interact with the aforementioned smart contracts, and *iii)* we used a relayer for withdrawing ETH on behalf of the authorized user. Finally, *iv)* a dApp was developed to collect votes.

---

[18] FollowMyVote.com: https://followmyvote.com.
[19] TIVI: https://tivi.io.
[20] MultiChain is a bridging platform for cryptocurrencies and NFTs across blockchains.

Possible future developments of what described in this paper concern the improvement of some of already incorporated functionalities: For instance, we would like to implement a Web dApp, which allows a user to connect their Meta-Mask account and then interact with the smart contract pools by performing deposits and withdrawals. In addition, we would like to enforce more properties from those presented in Sect. 2.3 *Confidentiality* and *Lack of evidence*, for example by implementing the project through the use of a permissioned blockchain, where the right to read the blockchain is granted only to certain users at certain times, so that they can count the votes once the voting is over [4]. Since we are not die-hard supporters of permissioned ledgers, one more option could be to obfuscate sensitive data, as the variables representing the number of currents votes for each candidate are [15].

Moreover, we plan to integrate the application with stronger schemes of authentication and authorization, such as OAuth and OpenID protocols. Finally, while on-chain confidentiality is ensured by Tornado Cash itself, before and after transactions are executed, the privacy of a voter may not be ensured when transactions are sent over the Internet. For this reason, we plan to extend the application by running it in an overlay network such as TOR.[21]

Acknowledgement. The authors are a member of the INdAM Research group GNCS and Consorzio CINI. This work has been partially supported by:
- GNCS-INdAM, CUP E55F22000270001;
- Project RACRA - funded by Ricerca di Base 2018–2019, University of Perugia;
- Project BLOCKCHAIN4FOODCHAIN: funded by Ricerca di Base 2020, University of Perugia;
- Project DopUP - REGIONE UMBRIA PSR 2014–2020;
- Project GIUSTIZIA AGILE, CUP: J89J22000900005.

References

1. Ahn, B.: Implementation and early adoption of an ethereum-based electronic voting system for the prevention of fraudulent voting. Sustainability **14**(5) (2022). https://doi.org/10.3390/su14052917. https://www.mdpi.com/2071-1050/14/5/2917
2. Alvarez, R.M., Hall, T.E., Trechsel, A.H.: Internet voting in comparative perspective: the case of Estonia. PS: Polit. Sci. Polit. **42**(03), 497–505 (2009)
3. Ayed, A.B.: A conceptual secure blockchain-based electronic voting system. Int. J. Netw. Secur. Appl. **9**(3), 1–9 (2017)
4. Bistarelli, S., Mercanti, I., Santancini, P., Santini, F.: End-to-end voting with non-permissioned and permissioned ledgers. J. Grid Comput. **17**(1), 97–118 (2019). https://doi.org/10.1007/s10723-019-09478-y
5. Buterin, V.: Ethereum white paper: a next generation smart contract & decentralized application platform (2013). https://github.com/ethereum/wiki/wiki/White-Paper

---

[21] https://docs.tornado.cash/general/how-to-use-tornado-cash-with-tor.

6. Fouard, L., Duclos, M., Lafourcade, P.: Survey on electronic voting schemes (2007). http://citeseerx.ist.psu.edu/viewdoc/download?doi=10.1.1.295.7959&rep=rep1&type=pdf. Verimag technical report. Accessed 28 Jan 2018

7. Hardwick, F., Akram, R.N., Markantonakis, K.: E-voting with blockchain: an e-voting protocol with decentralisation and voter privacy. CoRR abs/1805.10258 (2018). http://arxiv.org/abs/1805.10258

8. Loeber, L.: E-voting in the Netherlands; from general acceptance to general doubt in two years. In: Electronic Voting, vol. 131, pp. 21–30 (2008)

9. McCorry, P., Shahandashti, S.F., Hao, F.: A smart contract for boardroom voting with maximum voter privacy. In: Kiayias, A. (ed.) FC 2017. LNCS, vol. 10322, pp. 357–375. Springer, Cham (2017). https://doi.org/10.1007/978-3-319-70972-7_20

10. Mote, C.D.: Report of the national workshop on internet voting: issues and research agenda. In: Proceedings of the 2000 Annual National Conference on Digital Government Research, pp. 1–59. Digital Government Society of North America (2000)

11. Omohundro, S.: Cryptocurrencies, smart contracts, and artificial intelligence. AI Matters 1(2), 19–21 (2014)

12. Pilkington, M.: Blockchain technology: principles and applications. In: Research Handbook on Digital Transformations, p. 225 (2016)

13. Pramulia, D., Anggorojati, B.: Implementation and evaluation of blockchain based e-voting system with Ethereum and Metamask. In: 2020 International Conference on Informatics, Multimedia, Cyber and Information System (ICIMCIS), pp. 18–23 (2020). https://doi.org/10.1109/ICIMCIS51567.2020.9354310

14. Schneider, A., Meter, C., Hagemeister, P.: Survey on remote electronic voting. arXiv preprint arXiv:1702.02798 (2017)

15. Suegami, S.: Smart contracts obfuscation from blockchain-based one-time program. IACR Cryptology ePrint Archive, p. 549 (2022). https://eprint.iacr.org/2022/549

16. Swan, M.: Blockchain: Blueprint for a New Economy. O'Reilly Media, Inc. (2015)

Linking Contexts from Distinct Data Sources in Zero Trust Federation

Masato Hirai[✉], Daisuke Kotani, and Yasuo Okabe

Kyoto University, Yoshida-Honmachi, Sakyo-ku, Kyoto 606-8501, Japan
hirai@net.ist.i.kyoto-u.ac.jp

Abstract. An access control model called Zero Trust Architecture
(ZTA) has attracted attention. ZTA uses information of users and
devices, called context, to verify access requests. Zero Trust Federation
(ZTF) has been proposed as a framework for extending an idea of identity
federation to support ZTA. ZTF defines CAP as the entity that collects
context and provides it to each organization (Relying Party; RP) that
needs context for verification based on ZTA. For precise verification,
CAPs need to collect context from various data sources. However, ZTF
did not provide a method for collecting context from data sources other
than RP. In this research, as a general model for collecting context in
ZTF, we propose a method of linking identifiers between the data source
and CAP. This method provides a way to collect context from some
of such data sources in ZTF. Then, we implemented our method using
RADIUS and MDM as data sources and confirmed that their contexts
could be collected and used.

Keywords: Access control · Context · Zero trust

1 Introduction

In Zero Trust Architecture (ZTA) [7], an organization always verifies the origin
of access using data called context and authorizes access using the verification
results. Context includes continuously changing information such as the location
of the user or device, access history, as well as the surrounding conditions of
the accessing source. Context should be collected from various data sources for
precise verification.

To extend ZTA for Identity Federation(IdF), Zero Trust Federation (ZTF) [2]
is proposed as a model to extend ZTA to make authorization decisions using the
context of multiple organizations in IdF. The ZTF introduces Context Attribute
Provider (CAP) as an entity to share context in the federation. CAP collects
context independently of the organizations and provides context to each organization (Relying Party; RP) with the user's authorization. However, ZTF did not
provide the method of CAPs collecting context from sources other than RPs.
To make more precise authorization decisions in ZTF, it needs to collect diverse
contexts from more data sources, including those other than RPs.

© Springer Nature Switzerland AG 2023
A. Saracino and P. Mori (Eds.): ETAA 2022, LNCS 13782, pp. 136–144, 2023.
https://doi.org/10.1007/978-3-031-25467-3_9

The data sources that can provide context are diverse. For the data source to work as CAP, a huge amount of additional implementations are required, including communication with an authorization server to obtain the user's authorization status and sending the context to the RP. These implementations are not always possible for some data sources. Designing for each case would increase the cost of implementation, making it difficult to collect context from various data sources.

This study discusses the methods of collecting context to show the desirable architecture as a CAP, and proposes design for data sources that are difficult to make additional implementaion, which requires particular consideration.

The relationship between data source and CAP was unclear although CAP was proposed to collect and provide context in [2]. Therefore, we transfer CAP's role of collecting context to data sources and define the data sources as Context Collector (CtxC). This leaves the CAP's role only to provide contexts, and what we should discuss is how to send context from CtxC to the CAP. Contexts collected by CtxC usually contain the CtxC's unique user or device identifier (CtxC-id). For the CAP to provide the context received from CtxC to each RP, the CAP must determine to which user or device in CAP the context should be mapped. Thus, the problem is how to map the CtxC-id in the context to an identifier in the CAP(CAP-id). This study refers to this as linking context.

In this study, we propose a design for CtxC to perform the linking context in three cases: (1) a case where CtxC is easy to be extended for pseudonymous ID sharing with CAP, which was proposed in the previous ZTF; (2) a case where the administrator of CtxC and CAP is the same, which does not require additional implementation but trusts the administrators of both CtxC and CAP; (3) a case where CtxC uses certificates to authenticate devices or users, which does not require to trust the administrator links contexts properly. In (1), the CtxC and CAP share a pseudonymous ID for each user or device in advance, and the CtxC includes the pseudonymous ID in the context before sending it to the CAP so that the CAP can link the context to CAP-id. In (2), the administrator confirms the correspondence between identifiers in CtxC and CAP directly and places the correspondence table of the identifiers in CAP. In (3), CAP requests the certificate used in CtxC from the user or device and links identifiers which are related to the same certificates.

Furthermore, as a specific design for case (3), this study presents implementations for authentication and authorization by verifying factors such as which LAN the device is connected to and whether the device's OS has been compromised. As in CtxC, one implementation uses a RADIUS server using EAP-TLS and the other uses MDM. Through these implementations, we show the way of linking contexts using certificates.

2 Related Research

ZTA [7] is a new access control model in contrast to the traditional access control method, the perimeter model. ZTA controls access by continuously verifying access requests. To verify access, ZTA uses context, which includes static information as well as dynamic information such as the situation surrounding the user or device.

ZTF [2] is a framework for IdFs to federate the context to authenticate and authorize users like ZTA. ZTA typically has a single organization centrally collecting context [3]. However, in IdFs, contexts are dispersed across multiple RPs and cannot be aggregated. Therefore, ZTF defines Context Attribute Provider (CAP), which collects and provides context across IdFs. CAP is proposed as an entity that enables authentication and authorization using sufficient types and amounts of context, even for IdFs accessed infrequently.

As a method for CAP to provide context to the RP, ZTF proposes using CAEP [9] for continuous authentication and authorization and UMA [4] to authorize access under user's authorization.

However, it was unclear in the ZTF how to collect context from sources other than RPs. Collecting various contexts from sources including non-RP will improve authorization quality and will be required. For example, by using records of entering and leaving a room as context, it is possible to know where users are. On the other hand, the system of collecting such records does not provide a way of authenticating users directly via network. If the system is designed with different authentication requirements, it is too difficult to implement such authentication features. Therefore, the same protocols cannot be used as RPs when sharing a context with the RP.

3   The Method of Linking Context

3.1   Definition of Context Collector(CtxC)

Context is collected by RPs and CAPs in ZTF, but there are important data sources that belong neither to RP nor CAP. In order for such data source to be a CAP, the data source must manage the context based on the user's authorization to provide the context to the RP. However, these features are not implementable for all data sources, such as embedded systems. Therefore, to pursue a more desirable architecture, we define a data source as a Context Collector (CtxC). This means that we separate CAP's roles into collection and provision of context, and transfer the collection role to CtxC. In other words, CtxC is responsible for collecting the context, and CAP is responsible for verifying the user's authorization and providing the context to the RP. We redefine the CAP as always collecting context indirectly from the CtxC.

This change in ZTF is illustrated in Fig. 1. CAP2 receives the context indirectly from CtxC1. Also, RP2 is regarded as CtxC because it collects context directly from the user. A single CAP handles one or more CtxCs.

The Reason Why Linking Context is Necessary
When CtxC collects contexts, a user or a device that the contexts express is usually identified with CtxC's user/device identifier (CtxC-id). In contrast to CtxC-id, we call the identifier of the user in CAP as CAP-id. CAP must check the mapping between CtxC-id and CAP-id to manage user's authorization of

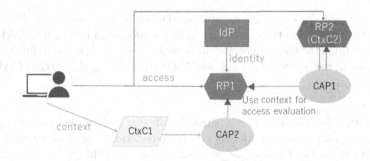

Fig. 1. ZTF organized by defining CtxC

RPs. Once CAP obtains that mapping, it can manage authorization status using such protocols as OAuth2.0 and UMA. Thus, to provide the context for RPs properly, CAP needs a method of mapping between the CtxC-id and the CAP-id. We call this mapping as linking context, and discuss the method of linking context. Since it is difficult to link context without making any assumptions about CtxC or CtxC-id, we considered three cases based on real use cases. We propose solutions for each of the cases below. One is the case where CtxC is easily extensible to share IDs using some protocols as in web applications. Another is the case where CtxC and the CAP administrator are the same. This case will be applicable for the entry/exit record system in a company. The other is the case where CtxC authenticates with client certificates. This case can apply to Radius server using EAP-TLS [8].

3.2   Linking Context

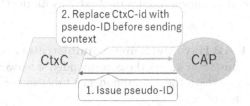

Fig. 2. The case where CtxC is easily extensible

When CtxC is Easily Extensible. In this case, we assume CtxC is so extensible that it can share pseudonymous ID. This is applicable for web applications. OpenID Connect (OIDC) [6] and SAML [5] are known as protocols for use of pseudonymous IDs.

The way of linking contexts is explained in Fig. 2. First, CAP issues a pseudonymous identifier (pseudo-ID) to CtxC. At this time, CAP stores the correspondence between the pseudo-ID and a CAP-id, and CtxC stores the correspondence between the pseudo-ID and a CtxC-id. The issue of pseudo-IDs can be implemented, for example, using OpenID Connect ID tokens [6]. CtxC then replaces the CtxC-id in the context with the pseudo-ID and sends it to CAP. This procedure allows the CAP to receive contexts with pseudo-IDs and to link contexts easily. Also, in this procedure, CtxC and CAP are exchangeable so that CtxC may issue pseudo-ID.

When CtxC is Not Easily Extensible. In this and subsequent sections, we will discuss methods of linking contexts in consideration of cases where CtxC is not easily extensible. In this case, we assume that no additional implementation to current implementation, such as embedded systems, can be made. For CtxC and CAP to share a pseudo-ID, CtxC must authenticate the user via a browser or native application to map the pseudo-ID and CtxC-id. Doing this would require additional implementation on CtxC's authentication for users or devices. However, this additional implementation is not realistic for this case.

Therefore, in this study, we have designed the CtxC to implement additionally only a feature of transmitting context to CAP, which is independent of the existing CtxC's implementation.

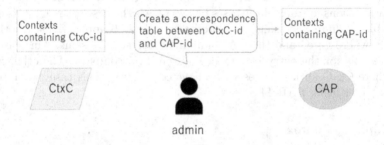

Fig. 3. Administrator associates the CtxC-id with the CAP-id.

When CtxC and CAP Have the Same Administrator. As shown in Fig. 3, in this case, the administrator knows the correspondence between a CtxC-id and a CAP-id so they can create the correspondence table in the CAP. CAP uses this table to link contexts.

For example, suppose that a company operates CAP and that the company would manage an entrance control system using IC cards as CtxC. When registering an IC card at the time of joining the company, the administrator creates a correspondence between the IC card identifier and the employee ID and registers it in the CAP, so that the CAP can easily link the context.

With this approach, it is only necessary to transmit the context from CtxC to CAP in some way, and little additional implementation is required. However, in this method, the CAP must trust that the administrator will maintain the correspondence table constantly.

When CtxC Authenticates Using Certificates. The method above requires implicit trust that the administrator will not link wrong context. Therefore, we propose a method of linking contexts without implicitly trusting the administrator. In this case, we assume the CtxC uses certificates for authentication and can send the correspondence between a certificate and CtxC-id to CAP with context. We also assume that the CA issues certificates correctly. Examples of certificates available in this proposal are X.509 certificates and certificates stored in IC cards that control entering/exiting rooms.

Fig. 4. Overview of authentication by certificate

In this assumption, CAP should verify the user/device has the private key of the certificate that the user/device uses for authentication in CtxC. The method is illustrated in Fig. 4.

We provide an overview in Fig. 4. As shown by the green arrow, CtxC requests a certificate from the user/device and authenticates using it. Then, CtxC sends the certificate and context to CAP. The CAP then requests the same certificate from the user/device used in CtxC to verify that the user/device has the certificate's private key. It also verifies that the certificate has not been modified by validating the certificate chain. This procedure allows the CAP to link contexts corresponding to certificates.

In this design, little additional implementation in CtxC is required. Only the feature of sending contexts to the CAP is needed. Also, we explained that the context is sent from CtxC to CAP, our method is applicable for a case where CtxC prepares an API and CAP obtains the context from it.

4   An Example of CtxC and CAP Implementation

As example implementations to collect context from CtxC, this section shows how CAP links context with the certificates, using 802.1X [1] RADIUS server and a MDM service. This implementation is published on GitHub[1].

In this scenario, we consider the RADIUS server and MDM as CtxC. The RADIUS server can collect connection logs in LAN and MDM can collect devices'

---

[1] https://github.com/laft2/cap-demo.

states. The connection logs have the information such as which access point the device connects, and are useful to locate the device. Also, the devices' states have the information such as whether the device's OS has no known vulnerabilities. The RP can use these pieces of information as context to control access precisely.

We implemented the method of using certificates, which is explained in Sect. 3. In our implementation, the Radius server authenticates devices using 802.1X EAP-TLS [8] and the MDM manages device certificates. These satisfy the assumptions as CtxCs in that method. Each CtxC sends a correspondence between context and certificate to the CAP, and the CAP links contexts by the certificate.

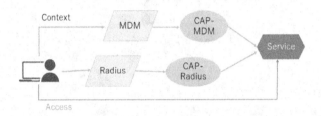

Fig. 5. Overview of implement

Figure 5 shows an overview of our implementation. As CtxCs, the Radius server sends connection logs to CAP-Radius and the MDM sends devices' states to CAP-MDM. They also send certificates with the context to CAPs. The CAP then requests the device with certificate used in CtxC to link the context. Afterward, the CAP associates the certificate with the CAP-id of the device. These procedures allow the CAP to provide the RP with the context obtained from CtxC.

In this implementation, we used the FreeRADIUS server in our laboratory as CtxC. Also, we used a Wi-Fi access point in the laboratory as an 802.1X authenticator. The Radius server controls access for the Wi-Fi access point to use EAP-TLS as an authentication protocol. For the CAP-Radius implementation, we used the Go and Echo, a web framework for Go.

We monitored and sent two files, one is the RADIUS authentication log, and the other is the accounting log. We have used fields of TLS-Client-Cert-Serial and TLS-Client-Cert-Issuer in the authentication logs. The CAP-Radius can authenticate the device and link the context using these pieces of information. From the accounting logs, we have used the field of Acct-Status-Type, which has the change of device's connectivity status as context. We also have used the fields of Acct-Input-Octets and Acct-Output-Octets, which express the device's traffic. We implemented CAP-Radius to turn these contexts into useful states such as whether the device is connected now.

We designed the CAP-Intune to gain context by periodically accessing Microsoft Intune's Managed Device API[2]. Intune is Microsoft's MDM service. We have used the fields of osVersion, complianceState, lostModeState, and jail-Broken to confirm that the device is securely maintained. For example, we can use the OS version to know if the device is known as a non-compromised OS. We implemented the ZTF using this information as a context.

5 Concluding Remarks

Zero Trust Federation (ZTF) [2] is a framework for authentication and authorization in ZTA under IdF. To clarify the relationship between CAP and the data source, we separate CAP's roles into the collection and provision of context, and transfer the collection role to other entity we define as CtxC. This separate leaves the CAP's role only to provide context. We clarifies that the problem for CAP to obtain the context from CtxC is that the CAP must obtain a correspondence between the CtxC-id and CAP-id. It is difficult to achieve this without making any assumptions. Therefore, we addressed this problem in three cases based on use cases: when additional implementation is easy like web applications, when the administrators of the CtxC and the CAP are the same like recorders of enter/exit the rooms, and when the CtxC authenticates with a certificate like Radius servers using EAP-TLS. Furthermore, we implemented the proposed method for the case where the RADIUS server and Intune are CtxC. This implementation specifically shows the method of linking contexts when CtxC uses certificates for authentication.

The only context available by the proposed method is for cases where CtxC satisfies certain assumptions. The availability of more diverse contexts is essential for making precise authorization decisions to more robustly protect resources. Therefore, in future work, further methods should be devised to allow RPs to use CtxC contexts with a wider range of conditions.

References

1. IEEE standard for local and metropolitan area networks-port-based network access control. IEEE STD 802.1X-2020 (Revision of IEEE STD 802.1X-2010 Incorporating IEEE STD 802.1Xbx-2014 and IEEE Std 802.1Xck-2018), pp. 1–289 (2020). https://doi.org/10.1109/IEEESTD.2020.9018454
2. Hatakeyama, K., Kotani, D., Okabe, Y.: Zero trust federation: sharing context under user control towards zero trust in identity federation. In: 2021 IEEE International Conference on Pervasive Computing and Communications Workshops and other Affiliated Events (PerCom Workshops), pp. 514–519 (2021). https://doi.org/10.1109/PerComWorkshops51409.2021.9431116
3. Kindervag, J., et al.: Build Security Into Your Network's DNA: The Zero Trust Network Architecture, vol. 27. Forrester Research Inc. (2010)

---

[2] https://docs.microsoft.com/ja-jp/graph/api/resources/intune-devices-manageddevice?view=graph-rest-beta.

4. Maciej Machulak, J.R.: Federated authorization for user-managed access (UMA) 2.0, Januray 2018. https://docs.kantarainitiative.org/uma/wg/rec-oauth-uma-federated-authz-2.0.html. Accessed 1 Feb 2022
5. OASIS Security Services TC: Security assertion markup language (SAML) v2.0 technical overview, March 2008. https://www.oasis-open.org/committees/download.php/27819/sstc-saml-tech-overview-2.0-cd-02.pdf
6. OpenID Foundation: Final: OpenID connect core 1.0 incorporating errata set 1, November 2014 https://openid.net/specs/openid-connect-core-1_0.html. Accessed 27 Jan 2022
7. Rose, S., Borchert, O., Mitchell, S., Connelly, S.: Zero trust architecture. NIST SP 800-207, September 2019. https://nvlpubs.nist.gov/nistpubs/SpecialPublications/NIST.SP.800-207-draft.pdf
8. Simon, D., Hurst, R., Aboba, D.B.D.: The EAP-TLS Authentication Protocol. RFC 5216, March 2008. https://doi.org/10.17487/RFC5216, https://www.rfc-editor.org/info/rfc5216
9. Tulshibagwale, A.: Re-thinking federated identity with the continuous access evaluation protocol, February 2019. https://cloud.google.com/blog/products/identity-security/re-thinking-federated-identity-with-the-continuous-access-evaluation-protocol

Author Index

Printed in the United States
by Baker & Taylor Publisher Services

Printed in the United States
by Baker & Taylor Publisher Services